Home Conversions

THE COMPLETE HANDBOOK

PAUL HYMERS

NEW HOLLAND

DEDICATION
For Melanie,
in particular the bit about jigsaw puzzles

Reprinted in 2004
First published in 2003 by New Holland Publishers (UK) Ltd
Garfield House, 86–88 Edgware Road
London W2 2EA
United Kingdom
London • Cape Town • Sydney • Auckland
www.newhollandpublishers.com

ISBN 1 84330 352 3

Senior Editor: Clare Sayer
Editor: Ian Kearey
Designer: Casebourne Rose Design Associates
Illustrator: Sue Rose
Cover photograph: Hannah Mornement

Printed and bound by Kyodo Printing Co (Singapore) Pte Ltd

ACKNOWLEDGEMENTS

Encouragement is always welcome, especially when it's from your children. Special
thanks to my daughters Karina and Rochelle.

Thanks as always to colleagues, past and present, for sharing with me their
knowledge and experience, in particular my old Building Control team of Darryl,
Robbo, Paula and Debby – the finest kind.

The publishers would like to thank Peta Smith and Plus1 Developments for
their help with the cover photography.
Plus1 Developments can be contacted on 07961 442849.

DECLARATION
The views expressed in this book are those of the author and do not necessarily
reflect those of his employers.

Contents

4 **Introduction**

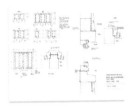

SECTION 1 **Planning**

6 *Chapter 1* Preliminaries

16 *Chapter 2* Plans

40 *Chapter 3* Builders

SECTION 2 **Converting**

59 *Chapter 4* Lofts

104 *Chapter 5* Basements

124 *Chapter 6* Garages

142 *Chapter 7* Barns and Outbuildings

170 Glossary

172 Useful Contacts

174 Index

Introduction

Night-time. Twenty-two thousand miles above the world. The lights of civilisation twinkle below, drawing out the shape of human settlement on the dark surface of the earth. From this distance at this time, civilisation is marked simply as white on black.

Images like these from geo-stationary satellites are commonplace now. You can buy posters of them, view them live over the Internet, they even make jigsaw puzzles of them. A puzzle made from this image of Europe would be a challenge, except possibly for one bit – Britain is going to be an easy piece to find, largely because at night it is one big white blob, centred on the south-east, but spreading out to the Midlands and much more.

This built-up island of ours is home to over 58 million people, all looking for space for themselves, space in which to live. But before we build over every field and woodland with newer and bigger homes, we can look to make better use of the space we already have, and what better place to start than in our lofts, basements, garages and outbuildings. This book is a guide that will help you to redesign and convert these spaces into liveable rooms, a task that for most will prove significantly cheaper than extending the home at ground level.

Whether you aim to do some of the work yourself or employ designers, builders and tradesmen to realise your plans for a larger, better and more valuable home, this practical and informative book will help you along the way.

At least that's the plan.

CHAPTER 1

Preliminaries

Home conversions

Conversion work is primarily the re-use of existing space, whether that space is currently redundant and simply waiting to be put to good use, or whether it is already employed but for the wrong purpose. More often than not, our homes aren't overburdened with redundant space these days, but they do have areas that could be put to better use and their potential maximised. If you are fortunate enough to live in an old property with a basement or out-building, the opportunities for conversion may be obvious, but for those of us occupying modern homes, it is a case of remodelling the space we have and putting it to the best possible use.

Converting lofts, garages and basements into living space is the most efficient way of maximising the potential of your home. Conversions have the added attraction of not losing valuable garden space, which in modern homes tends to be at a premium anyway. Not only that, but they are normally the most economical option, even comparing favourably, per square metre, with conservatories, which have now peaked in popularity and become almost as expensive as conventional extensions.

Having to create extra living space in our homes might have been avoided if we had been building them for the last 50 years with loft and basement rooms. But we haven't; if anything, we have been building homes that are awkward to create extra space in, not because we want them that way but because it is a seller's market and as a developer, you can build low-cost, low-quality homes and sell them at high prices.

A 2001 survey carried out by the Traditional Housing Bureau on what consumers wanted from new housing, revealed that 44 per cent of people questioned would like a room in the roof and 43 per cent a basement room. The vast majority wanted some decent sound insulation, not only between houses, but also within them, and this was reported as being the most important construction factor. The survey proved one thing – that we are interested in knowing how the property was built and with what materials. Not surprising really – if you bought a new car you might want to look at its specification first, and performance and build quality would be an issue, along with the price.

So why haven't developers built in loft rooms from the start? In short, it is too much hassle for them, and they can make money far more efficiently by using standard roof trusses. It has been calculated that it would add less than 10 per cent to the cost of an average four-bedroom detached house to provide a room in the roof. Alas, developers seem sceptical that the customer would be prepared to pay that extra. But in certain areas where it has been done, loft rooms have added 30 per cent to the value of homes.

So there is money to be made from utilising roof space. It needn't be your first priority, but property developers do very well from buying up bungalows and converting their lofts, and any home improvement carried out well will add value to your home.

A better use

Converted living space tends to be used flexibly. A loft room may be a study space, home office or guest bedroom at different times – likewise a converted basement, with its cool temperature and good sound insulation, may make an ideal dining room for entertaining or a playroom for the children. With today's advanced home-entertainment systems, I can think of no better use for a converted basement than as a home cinema or music room.

Few lofts or basements are converted solely into bathrooms, but if that is what you're planning, some careful consideration of drainage is essential before you go too far. It may be that your basement is below the level of the outside drains and can only be served by a fully pumped system. Issues like these are not insurmountable, but they will bear on the cost of the work and so it is paramount to start your project with a proper assessment. Look at what you want to gain from the space and what will be necessary to get you there.

Investigation and preparation

To begin with, you should look at your home and its potential – the nature of the space you are about to convert, and what possible problems, if any, it holds for you. You may think you know your own home, but are you sure you know which are the supporting walls inside or where the water main runs, or where the soil and vent pipe is? These things will have a bearing on what you can use the space for and how your conversion can be designed, approved and built.

So before you think about appointing an architect or a builder, find out as much as you can yourself about the construction of your home and where the services lie. Make some notes – they will prove useful later on when you begin to plan your conversion.

Load-bearing walls

For loft conversions it is essential that you check out the load-bearing elements of your home. Most importantly, and even if you do nothing else, dig a small hole down alongside your outside wall, sufficiently deep to reveal the type and depth of your existing house foundations. It is likely that your building control officer will want to see them anyway, to establish their adequacy for the increased load.

If you can, try to establish where the load-bearing walls are inside. By load-bearing, I mean walls that were built from a foundation rather than just off the floor – normally that is any wall that is supporting something other than itself, such as floor joists, beams, ceiling or roof members. These load-bearing walls may need to be used in the design of your conversion to take some extra weight, and you can't have your designer or builder trying to load up walls that were never built to take the weight.

An added problem is that in some properties (such as some early-twentieth-century homes) the ceiling and even the roof may have been strutted down onto an internal wall built off the floor slab. In these cases a decision will have to be made as to whether the increase in load is enough to warrant doing anything about the matter.

10 Preliminary Points for Lofts

CONSIDER THESE TEN POINTS BEFORE
YOU BEGIN A LOFT CONVERSION:

1 HEADROOM

Make sure that your converted roof space will have enough height to give you comfortable headroom. You can do this by measuring the height inside the loft at present between the underside of the ridge (the apex of the roof) and the top of the joists. Alas, this dimension itself will not be your finished headroom, because inevitably new floor joists (that are much deeper than the existing ceiling joists) will have to be installed to take the floor. The depth of finishings, such as ceiling plasterboard and floorboarding, will also reduce it. As a rough guide you should take at least 200 mm off to allow for these elements, and a further 200 mm if you propose to build out a dormer window. In the latter case, this will allow for the depth of the dormer's flat roof joists and finishings, all of which must align beneath the existing ridge.

So what is normal headroom? Around 2.3 or 2.4 m is standard, but you certainly shouldn't go below 2 m. This is effectively door height, and any less will fail to meet the Building Regulations requirement for headroom on staircases, which applies to the landing space at the top as well as the flight. There is currently no headroom requirement for the room itself, but you have got to be able to stand up in there, and a low ceiling creates a claustrophobic effect if not a crick in the neck.

2 ROOF STRUCTURE

All roof structures are convertible, but some are easier to convert than others. In spite of what you may have read elsewhere, trussed rafter roofs can be converted and often are. What is important is the sequence in which the work is done. Roof pitch is relevant because it is related to headroom. Homes built after 1960 may have trussed

rafter roofs with a lower pitch, 30 degrees for example, that may mean that the headroom is just not enough. An 8-m-wide house with a 30-degree roof pitch will have less headroom than you think. Properties built before then with cut-and-pitched roofs are more likely to have steeper pitches, 40 to 50 degrees, and better headroom. Many homes built in the first half of the twentieth century with 50 x 100 mm rafters and purlin supports are ideal.

3 STAIRS
(a) Existing stairs from ground floor to first floor

In a two-storey house, the position of the stairs at present is important to loft conversions. Ideally they should descend to a lobby, porch or reception hall leading to an outside door, and not into a habitable room, like the lounge. If they do occur in a living room, it is likely that you will have to form either a hall or corridor wall linking the stairs to an outside door to enable safe escape in a fire, or construct a lobby with two doors at the base of the stairs, providing you with optional routes out through two different rooms.

All of these are fire safety issues that are covered by Building Regulations, and the options for alternatives are few and far between.

(b) New stairs from first floor to the loft room

Space will be at a premium, and ideally you need to bring new stairs up from the existing landing below, rather than from a room. If there isn't room for a normal staircase of 42 degrees maximum pitch, then you may have to consider a space-saver type stair with paddle treads, or even a fixed ladder access. Loft-room stairs can be narrower than normal, down to 600 mm wide, serving one room. The plan diagram on page 10 shows stair positioning in a loft conversion.

4 USE

What use do have in mind for your new loft room? A bathroom may not attract the full fire-safety requirements of the Building Regulations, but all other rooms will. Consider using the new space flexibly, for example, as a study or home office with the advantage of becoming a guest bedroom.

Look to maximise the storage space in the design and by carefully choosing the furniture you put in.

5 WINDOWS

Give some thought to the type of windows you would like. Dormer windows that project out expand on the maximum headroom space, and where headroom is tight, they are essential.

Rooflights that sit within the pitch of the roof are cheaper and create far better day lighting, but do nothing to expand on the available headroom.

6 STORAGE SPACE

Look to build in cupboards because inevitably some or all of your room will have sloping ceilings that shop furniture will not fit to. Built-in wardrobe and stowage drawers are easy to include and will maximise the available space.

7 ROOM LAYOUT

Consider the room layout of your house at present. The route out should ideally pass down through the house without needing to pass through habitable rooms. The existing doors to the rooms will need self-closing devices in your finished three-storey home.

8 DRAINS

If you are planning to provide bathroom facilities in your loft, locate the position of the existing SVP or soil pipe serving the drains. This will need to be extended and connected into, and will have a bearing on where your new appliances can go.

9 HOT WATER

Even if you aren't providing new hot-water services to the loft room, you will probably be relocating the existing ones. Water tanks will have to be repositioned and pipes moved. If you need a hot-water supply up here for a bath, basin or shower, it will be necessary to find a more elevated position for the tanks than the appliances, or perhaps switch to a combination boiler.

10 STABILITY

Of course the work will need to be carried out and completed with structural stability, and an engineer's calculated design will ensure this, but also you need to spare a moment to consider whether your home is at present structurally strong enough to take the increased weight that is made by a loft conversion.

Look for signs of settlement, dig a small hole outside to view the depth and spread of the foundations, and try to establish the nature of lintels you have above the windows. Ultimately these issues will be dealt with by your designer, builder or Building Control Officer (or all three), but if you suspect a problem at present, now would be a good time to have it checked out, rather than later.

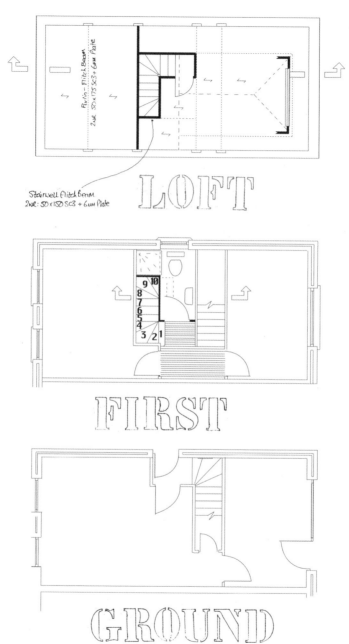

Purlin – Flitch Beam
2nr. 50 x 175 SC3 + 6mm Plate

Stairwell Flitch Beam
2nr: 50 x 150 SC3 + 6mm Plate

LOFT

FIRST

GROUND

Plans – loft conversion floor layouts.

Services

Where are the electricity or gas meters, water and phone entry points? The relevant service companies will be able to give you the location of their pipes and ducts, either by an on-site survey or plan. Drainage should also be investigated. Local authorities hold records of public sewers but not private drains. Only site surveys can trace them accurately, and coloured vegetable dyes mixed with water are useful in finding out what goes where.

If you suspect that you have some buried services, many service companies – gas, electricity, water and telephone – now offer a free site survey to determine the exact position of their service pipes. They are able to do this by using sensitive detection equipment – although you might be just as good with a dowsing rod. In the past, they have only been able to issue marked-up location plans, which were often inaccurate. If you can't get a site survey done and have to settle for a plan or nothing at all, then beware and proceed carefully.

Drainage

If your converted space includes a bathroom, WC or kitchen, you are going to need access to your drainage system for the new appliances, so this is the time to investigate where your drains are and where they run to. Although previous plans can be of some help here, the only sure way to find out is to lift manhole covers and measure depths from the bottom of the channel to the cover. Needless to say, it is absolutely necessary to ensure that your existing drains are deep enough to allow any new pipes to be connected at a reasonable fall, and that the connection can be made in the general direction of the flow, or at least at no less than 90 degrees to it.

For 'emergency' situations there are mini-pumped systems which will allow extra toilets and other appliances to be installed where it is not possible to supply conventional drains. Because the pumps run on electricity, these systems should only be used where you have other conventional WCs and facilities that dispose of foul water in the standard way, by gravity.

Rain and wind

I confess to being a bit excited when I first heard about global warming. I thought it meant we would be growing palm trees in the garden and spending more time on the beach. Apparently it doesn't – it means our winters are getting milder and wetter, the seasons blending together under the mild humid blanket of grey we call our weather. Stop me if I'm depressing you, but we have already seen what an increase of 0.7° Centigrade does to our climate, and we are told to expect a much higher rise in temperature over the next few decades.

In the year 2000 over a twelve-month period it rained more than it has ever rained in Britain since records were kept: 1299 mm over 52 weeks. Our building designs will have to change to deal with this soon; already brickwork walls are becoming saturated and poor detailing is leaving us vulnerable to the elements. We aren't just talking about a few minor damp patches either here –

we are talking about bucketloads of water simply penetrating our homes through the brick structure, around window and door openings, through chimneys and so on.

If you are the least bit suspicious about the exposure of your brickwork, it may be worth cladding it. Even if you only clad the most severely hit elevation, a weatherboarded or tiled wall will be an efficient rain screen. Make sure that your designer details the join to any brickwork below, as water can flow off large areas of cladding or glass and saturate these bricks if given half a chance.

Trees

If you wish to trim back a tree that is encroaching on the roof or new windows, you must first check to ensure that it does not have a Preservation Order placed upon it. Most local authority Planning Departments have a tree or landscape officer who can advise you if this is the case.

In Conservation Areas it is an offence to lop or top trees without obtaining the consent of the council and giving them six weeks' notice. The same also applies to uprooting or felling trees. Before you contact the council, note that it is not a

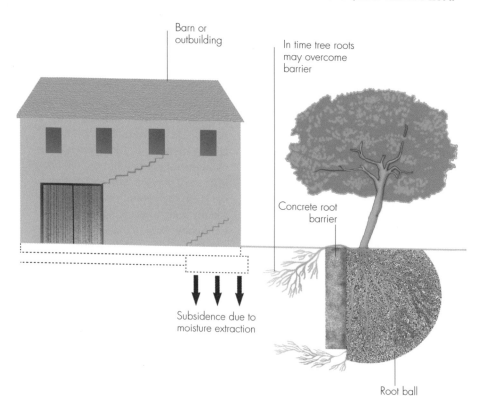

Installing a root barrier can slow down subsidence movement but may not prevent it.

sufficient defence to claim that your conversion would be affected by the tree if it was retained. Concrete root barriers can be used to restrict the growth of tree roots. A concrete wall about 1 m deep is built under ground to prevent or slow down root growth beyond the wall (see the diagram on page 12).

Flooding

For basement and garage conversions, and if you are new to the property, look to see if there any signs of past flooding or a high water table in evidence. Are you near to a river or on the coast? Consult with neighbours to find out the history of the area. Is the water table high? Flood damage to your home has to be one of the most destructive and disheartening things.

If your existing home has a low ground-floor level, do not feel you have to continue it into the converted garage, for example. If all you need to do is raise the floor level in your conversion by a few extra courses to be safe, it must be worth doing. Building the ground floor level higher in here may mean you are building a refuge. The Environment Agency is in the process of developing a national Geographical Information System (GIS) plan of areas at risk from flooding, so that home-owners in these areas may take precautions and design home improvements with flood protection in mind from the start.

Maps or advice from the Environment Agency are of some help when it comes to established flood plains, but with the increase in global warming, every year now seems to see record flooding in one or another part of the UK.

Maps

You may need a location plan for your planning application, and copies of scale 1:2500 or 1:1250 OS maps are only obtainable from certain outlets (including local authorities) who are licensed by Ordnance Survey to sell them, but they can also be viewed in most public libraries.

If there is any doubt as to where exactly the boundary of your property lies, then the Land Registry will provide a marked-up map on application (for a fee). Maps aren't too important with most conversion work, but for barns and outbuildings they could help you to date the building.

Restrictive covenants

These may exist on your land. Covenants* are clauses in a contract which was drawn up for the sale of the land previously and are binding on all future purchasers. They may require, for example, home-owners to seek consent from the original developer for any extension or alteration they wish to make to the property; in so doing, they aim to control the character of the estate as a whole. Covenants may prevent any building or conversion at all, so it is important to check the deeds of your property to ensure if any exist.

* Covenants may be removed by application to the Lands Tribunal under Section 84 of the Property Act 1925.

Wildlife displacement

Things have a habit of residing in basements and attics, and before you get to designing your conversion in full, you

10 Preliminary Points for Basements

TEN POINTS TO CONSIDER BEFORE YOU BEGIN A BASEMENT CONVERSION ARE:

1 DRAINAGE

If you are planning to provide a kitchen, utility room or bathroom facility in your newly converted basement, drainage will be an overriding issue. It is quite possible that your existing drains are too shallow to allow you to connect easily into them. Lift the manhole covers closest to the house and basement area and see what depth they are. Locate the SVP and note its position in relation to the basement. If the drains are too shallow to allow access, you will need a fully pumped waste system – and the most economical of these systems allows you to connect a 25-mm pipe waste to the SVP.

2 DAMP

Dampness is the reason why many basements are left unused. It can be overcome. There are plenty of tanking (damp-proofing) methods available today for basement walls and floors that can overcome the most extreme damp problems. If your problem isn't so much damp as flooding, then you will need to address the problem at least partially from outside the building where the water is coming in. Damp can be seasonal: just because the basement is dry in summer doesn't mean it will be in winter. Assess the walls and floor after a prolonged wet spell, preferably in the winter months, and make a note to advise your designer of the extent of the problem to be overcome.

3 STAIRS

As with loft stairs, space in basements can be at a premium and a fixed ladder or paddle-tread stair may have to be considered, but wherever possible look for a standard staircase or make a feature with spiral or helical stairs; the latter can be ideal for basements because they require larger stairwell openings in the floor, which helps to light the room and also opens it up to the ground floor.

4 LIGHT

Daylight for basements is not normally at a premium, and artificial lighting may have to be relied upon. If you can't provide even a high-level window to let in some natural light, you might wish to open the room up a bit to the house above or even install a daylight tube – a highly polished pipe with a lens at either end that can be built in to allow natural light through from the roof or outside wall.

5 VENTILATION

You may choose not to have any daylight, but you can't choose not to have any ventilation. All rooms require ventilation of some sort if they are to be useable. If windows aren't available or possible, then airbricks usually are (although you might need plenty of them); they can be installed like periscopes to duct air from the ground above. Mechanical extractor ventilation will be needed for wet rooms like kitchens, utility rooms and bathrooms, but it can also be designed to ventilate living space with at least three air changes per hour.

6 FLOOR

Is the existing floor level as well as dry? If it isn't it you may need to replace it with a new one. A concrete floor is essential with whatever finish you require, so long as it is damp-proof and level. A brick floor could be a reasonable alternative and will give the cellar some ambience, but it will require sealing both underneath and above to ensure durability.

7 USE

Decide early on what use you intend to have for your new underground room. Utility rooms for washing machines, tumble dryers and boilers are excellent places for the naturally sound-proofed basement.

Entertainment rooms are also popular for TV and surround-sound home-entertainment systems. Basements can also make ideal dining rooms with their cool temperature and potential for creative artificial lighting and imaginative design.

8 LAYOUT

Ideally, the basement stair should be accessed from the hallway or corridor at ground level above and not via another room. If it is the only route out of the home, a fire occurring in the room above may leave you trapped in the basement, unable to escape. A window serving the basement from a light-well outside could be considered as an optional escape route if it opened large enough for you to climb out.

9 STORAGE

As with loft conversions, storage is often lost when basements are converted, so remember to consider where else you can store things that would otherwise be down here. If possible, think about building in a walk-in cupboard.

10 INSULATION AND HEATING

Basements can retain a year-round cool temperature, and that may be what you require from your new room. If it isn't and you want to heat it, then you will also need to insulate it. Insulation can be installed to the existing walls before they are relined, and to a new floor by varying methods.

---

are going to have to ask them to leave. Certain species are protected by law under the Wildlife Act and cannot be disturbed. Others, such as mice, squirrels and wasps, are considered vermin and can be dealt with under the heading 'pest control'.

If you'd rather relocate wildlife than kill it, live traps can be set for mice and entry points sealed up after nests have been removed.

The next step in the process is to find somebody to prepare the plans, but only after they have visited your home and checked it for a feasibility study. Some surveyors and architects offer a brief appraisal free of charge, during which the findings from your site investigation can be discussed along with your design ideas and queries.

Preliminary work isn't just about exploring the fabric of your home, it's as much about where your home is and what sort of environment it's in. And these days much of this fact-finding can be done from the safety of your desktop.

CHAPTER 2

Plans

Finding a designer

For most conversion projects it is a good idea to employ someone to design the conversion work and deal with the local authority submissions for you. In the case of some minor conversions (such as integral garages to living space) you may be happy to deal with these yourself. Loft conversions, however, require a major design input that warrants a professional designer who is competent in both structural and architectural design and conversant with the requirements of the Building Regulations. Finding one person who fits this bill is not always possible and many architectural designers farm out the structural elements of their design to engineers, particularly as this part of the scheme usually needs justifying by structural calculations.

If you don't have the benefit of a personal recommendation from friends who have had similar work done, start by considering which professional institutions exist with suitably qualified members in your area. The difficulty is that designers of building work are not required to belong to any particular association or institute or possess any particular knowledge or skills. Hence the market is awash with 'designers' of varying qualification and ability.

Not only are there several bodies for designers to belong to, but there are usually different levels of membership based on their qualifications and experience, from student members who are training in the industry to fully qualified members and finally 'fellow

members' who are blessed with years of experience. My advice is to find somebody in the middle that is actively involved in designing your type of conversion on a regular basis.

Consider using a professional whose institute requires him or her to carry out a certain amount of continuing development rather than rest on their original qualifications. Some bodies also require their members to use a standardised 'terms of business' letter, setting out their terms and complaints handling procedures.

Although it has become a popular term for anyone drawing plans, some protection of the title 'architect' exists under law. Because of this, design professionals often refer to themselves as building consultants, architectural designers, surveyors, engineers or even technical consultants – anything but architects unless they are actually registered with the Architects Registration Board. To avoid confusion, I will refer to them as 'designers' throughout this book.

A good designer is one who possesses the necessary skills of draughtsmanship and is familiar not only with the details of construction, but also with the problems and regulations relating to the work. Don't make the mistake of thinking that someone who designs large-scale projects is more qualified to draw up plans for your garage conversion – it is more likely that a local 'plan draughtsman', who has worked on similar projects, is more qualified for the job in hand.

Here are a few examples of the institutes which designers may belong to:

Royal Institute of British Architects (RIBA)

This is the principal architects' club. Only those registered with the Architects Registration Board are entitled to use the declaration 'architect', which may explain why there are so many 'architectural technicians' around.

Royal Institution of Chartered Surveyors (RICS)

A widely recognised institute that covers a wide range of professions, from auctioneers and arbitrators to quantity surveyors. The only appropriate discipline for design work would be that of Building Surveyor, but often these are dedicated to valuation and structural surveys for property conveyance so look for one in the design market.

Association of Building Engineers (ABE)

A body whose members are principally building surveyors or building control surveyors with a sound knowledge in building technology and law.

Institute of Building (IOB)

A long-established body for members of the building industry, this is often patronised by non-trade employees of building contractors, such as site agents, contracts managers and so on.

Institute of Structural Engineers (ISE)

Some structural engineers may also prepare structural design plans as well as calculations, but generally they have no expertise outside of structures and would usually restrict their services to these elements. There is also an Institute of Civil Engineers (ICE), but often their field of structures is confined to roads, bridges, tunnels, etc., and is removed from conversion design.

Structural design work

One thing to remember with loft conversions is that at least half of the design work is structural and requires a structurally competent person. Most architectural designers are not insured or competent enough to carry out structural design work, so a structural engineer will need to be employed. His or her design calculations will resolve beam and joist sizes, fixing details and sometimes procedural information for the architectural designer to transfer onto the plans.

It is vitally important that the structural engineer's design conclusions are transferred onto the plans, as a builder will rely on these first. With loft conversions, do not consider employing an architectural designer to draw up working plans for Building Regulations submission if he or she is not including the structural design work. It is only half the job. If he or she isn't including design calculations and details with the plans, you will want to know if they will be appointing a structural engineer and what their charges are for this essential part of the job. Since the cost of structural calculations can be equal to, if not more than the cost of the plans, it is important that you resolve these issues before engaging anyone. Make sure that they are contained within a written contractual agreement between you.

So often, abortive work is carried out on loft and barn conversions because the builder has relied solely upon the

10 Ten Expert Points

LOOK FOR THE FOLLOWING TEN EXPERT POINTS IN FINISHED PLANS:

1 CLARITY

How clear and easy-to-read are they? Is the writing legible?

You may not understand what is written, but if it isn't printed clearly then neither will anybody else.

2 TRUE ELEVATIONS

Are there elevations of all aspects, showing the finished property as a whole, in addition to floor plans?

Elevations are the one aspect where the designer can display his artistic flair alongside his technical draughting abilities. Often well-drawn elevations can help to 'sell' the design.

SOUTH-WEST

NORTH-EAST

3 SCALE
Are they drawn to an appropriate scale – proposed plan layouts/elevations 1:50; sections 1:25; block plan 1:500; location plan 1:1250?

4 PLAN COPY SIZE
Are they reproduced on A1 or A0 size paper? Having to refer to several different sheets of smaller A3 or A4 paper during the work is not going to be helpful.

Note, however, that with structural design work or minor conversions (such as garages) some architects prefer to work on A3.

5 MEASUREMENTS
Are they annotated clearly with plenty of measurements in the same units (i.e. all in metric or imperial, not shared)? Internal dimensions for all walls, positions of windows and doors are most important, as are positions of supporting beams.

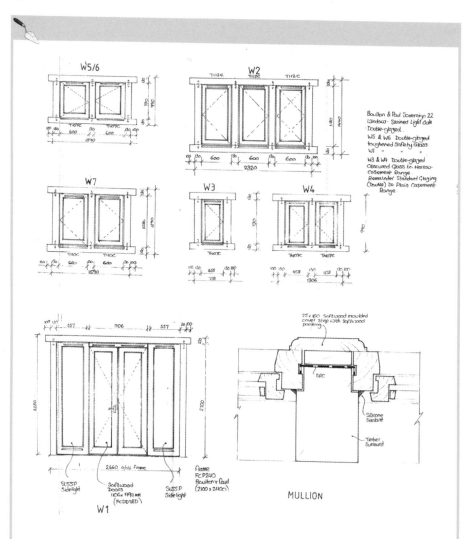

Boulton & Paul Sovereign 22
Window - Stained Light Oak
Double-glazed.
W5 & W6 Double-glazed
toughened Safety Glass.
W1   "   "   "
W3 & W4 Double-glazed
Obscured Glass to Narrow
Casement Range.
Remainder Standard Glazing
(Double) to Plain Casement
Range.

MULLION

SPECIFICATION

6 Are the Building Regulations plans comprehensive and detailed? Are they annotated with a detailed and bespoke specification? *Most importantly, do they tie up with the structural calculations?*

LEVELS AND HEADROOM

7 Do they show a true representation of the floor and outside ground levels, either as existing or as proposed? Do the sections indicate the headroom available between finishes in a loft at beneath the ridge, on the stairs and landing, and also beneath the lowest part of the ceiling? Some loft conversion package companies neglect to point out how much headroom is restricted (where you can't actually stand up).

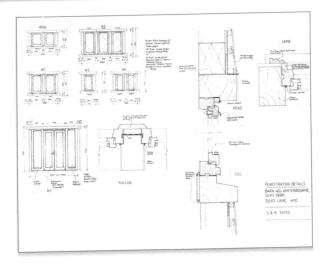

FENESTRATION DETAILS
BARN ADJ. WINTERBOURNE,
SILKS FARM,
SILKS LANE, WYE.

S. & K. YATES

8 DETAILS

Are there separate large-scale details of connections or critical areas of construction, such as rafter to ashlare wall connections, and connections between beams and joists or rafters?

9 RED HERRINGS

Are the plans free from statements like '...work to comply with Building Regulations – Approved Document...'? This is generally an indication that the designer is trying to palm off his responsibilities to the builder and avoiding having to detail some elements. You, the client, do not need to know what the references of the Building Regulations are, only that your scheme complies with them. Pre-printed standard specifications are also to be avoided. Some designers use this as a labour-saving tool, but it is far from helpful to their clients or the builders, since it usually contains some notes that will not apply to your project. All conversions are unique in some way and deserve a bespoke specification, free from bits that don't apply.

10 PRESENTATION

And finally, do the plans look as though they have been drawn with care and pride?

In other words, are they clear – have they been drawn with black drawing ink and in a variety of pen nib thicknesses? Do they show plenty of detail? Are they presentable, and are the notes printed and legible?

If you are happy that the plans satisfy all of the above points, then you might well be in the hands of a professional. Even so, it is still worth comparing the drawings of several designers before appointing one. You may be astonished to see just how different the quality of plans can be, and it will give you a good idea of the wide variety of drawing standards around.

architectural plans and not followed the engineer's calculations. To be fair, structural calculations are not always easy to understand, and unless they have been translated on to the drawings or spelt out in the written specification, builders will often overlook them.

The only sure way to prevent this from happening is to check for yourself that your engineer is happy that the structural design is represented on the final plans as well as in the calculations. Make both designer and engineer aware that you want a comprehensive and clear drawing indicating all of the structural work and the sequence in which it is to be carried out.

It is possible (and not uncommon) for an incompetent builder to render a home a dangerous structure through bad workmanship and the inability to follow structural designs. Loft conversions are not something that you can make up as you go along; they require careful design and careful implementation.

Most designers will offer a free consultation period, when they will visit your house to discuss with you the feasibility of extending it. Ask them to bring along to the meeting some examples of conversion plans drawn for their previous clients. Always view their work before agreeing any terms.

Agreeing the terms of engagement

Some professional bodies require their members to use a form of contract setting out the rules of their engagement. But even where they don't, establish some yourself and have them put in writing.

The most common area of complaint comes from the issue of structural calculations or details that may be required by Building Control as part of their submission. Some designers may not be entirely up-front about what their price does and does not include. They may even be adamant that calculations will not be needed, but if your scheme involves the conversion of a roof or timber-framed barn, it is likely that they will. This would apply whether it is timber or steel beams proposed and even perhaps when existing lintels and beams are to be retained.

Another cause for complaint arises when building work starts and queries with the design arise. Invariably the builder has to resolve issues with their clients and Building Control because the designers ceased to be involved once approvals were granted.

Most designers work on a fixed-fee basis that can be agreed before pen is put to paper, and it makes sense to know whether that fee will cover any minor amendments needed by planning or Building Control officers before approval is given. Usually you would expect their fee to contain an element of alteration or consultation work necessary to gain approvals. It might not, however, run to a full redrawing if you change your mind and want a bathroom in the basement instead of a bedroom, or the roof needs to be reconstructed to achieve adequate headroom. Hopefully, a professional will be able to anticipate shortfalls and problems and give you early warning of potential setbacks.

Establish whether the fee includes Planning and Building Regulations fees –

which are not insignificant – or whether you will be asked to pay these separately. In the eyes of the Local Authority the responsibility lies with the homeowner, and it would be to them that they look in the event of a bad debt. If you do agree that your designer pays the fees on your behalf, make it a written contract between the two of you – a statement jointly signed and copied would suffice and may save many arguments later.

Experienced and knowledgeable designers should be able to give you some warning of any possible problems with your requirements before they draw the scheme up. A professional designer will draw up the plans on a negative that can easily be amended by scratching out and reworking. Some local authorities require nothing more than a written note for a specification change, while others may insist upon amended plans – the latter are best to cover any design changes that take place.

If conditions are imposed on your approval, make sure that your designer resolves these conditions (which are usually listed on an attached schedule accompanying the plans approval notice) as soon as possible. Leaving them unaddressed until the work is underway can lead to problems.

Submitting your applications

There is one very important point to get across here, a point that is the cause of much angst and confusion to home-owners. Almost every book that mentions either Planning or Building Regulations seems to mix the two together or imply that they are linked, if not one and the same thing. They are not. The most they have in common is that their officers work in the same building. In truth the two disciplines are entirely separate and bear about as much resemblance to each other as Laurel and Hardy. **Approval from one does not constitute, in any shape or form, approval from the other.**

The forms used by local planning and building control authorities are intended for universal use, in other words they are the same whether you are applying to build a shopping mall or convert your garage to a playroom. Consequently, half of the questions will not seem entirely relevant or even understandable. If you aren't sure whether they apply or not, ask before submitting them.

Local authorities have to follow the legislation controlling their function, by setting out what is required to make a valid application. In 1999 the fees for Building Regulations were devolved from central government to local government, so that each authority could set its own fees necessary to make it self-financing and competitive. It hasn't made it any easier, and it certainly hasn't made it any cheaper. Designers can no longer assume that the fee they pay for similar applications in different districts will be the same. Hence designers themselves are frequently submitting the wrong fees with their work and delaying the approvals. If you've overpaid on the plan fee, some councils may say that the overpaid element will be deducted from your inspection fee when it is charged later rather than simply invalidate your application. If it's underpaid, they are likely to invalidate your application.

Check the following details before sending in your submission:

- The right information is on the forms, particularly the description, which will be reproduced on your approvals most likely word for word
- The correct number of plan and form copies are enclosed
- The application fee is correct
- The site plan is enclosed with the boundaries edged in red
- That there is a relevant amount of information on the plans for the type of submission you are making

Building Notice

As an alternative to a full plans application under the Building Regulations, a Building Notice is intended as an expedient way of making a formal application. It requires no plans or design details at all, just a name, address and description type of form. The problem is that it isn't an application at all. It is a legal statement to say what work you are going to be carrying out and that you will comply with the requirements of the Building Regulations when you do it, whatever they are. All of which is fine if you do know what they are and that your conversion will comply with them – because if you don't and it doesn't, you won't find out until the work is inspected, and by then it could be costly to alter it.

It is normally considered unwise to tackle a loft conversion this way, given lofts' dependence on thorough structural design. Consequently it is only advisable to adopt this procedure for minor conversions like garages, and only after discussing with your builder and Building

Control Surveyor the scheme in detail. That way they can agree on the details before each stage of the work.

If you are proposing to carry out the conversion yourself, it would be advisable to have an approved set of plans from which to work.

Building Warrants and Structural Design Certificates (Scotland)

In Scotland, where they write their own legislation, the system is slightly different to that in England and Wales. Building Warrants are applied for instead of approvals, but they amount to the same thing and some elements of the work can be self-certified. The most relevant of these is the Structural Design Certificate, which can be submitted by either a full or corporate member of the Institute of Civil Engineers (ICE) or the Institute of Structural Engineers (IStructE) as a statement of compliance in respect of structural stability.

As your agents, they are, in effect, self-certifying the structural design of the conversion work, rather than having to have it checked by another qualified engineer at the local authority. A 'supporting statement' must be submitted with the certificate regarding the stability of the property, in other words qualifying its adequacy for the extra weight of the conversion, and a new design certificate must be submitted for any later amendments affecting the structure. Plans showing the structural design are required to be submitted for reference with the conditions on which it is drawn. These conditions can be verified on site once the work has begun.

Local authority approvals and exemptions

The following gives an indication of some exemption categories. It is only a guide, because the law may change.

Planning Consent may or may not be required for your proposed conversion. A house which has not been extended before might still have **permitted development** rights which would allow you to do the work without needing Planning Consent. The law changes regularly, as to what constitutes permitted development and you should **always check with your local Planning Authority** and apply for a **Lawful Development Certificate** for your particular project. They will only do this on receipt of detailed plans and in some cases a fee.

Under the Town and Country Planning Act 1990 (General Development Order) current guidelines for Permitted Development of domestic conversions in England and Wales are as follows Variations in Scotland under the Town and Country Planning (General Permitted Development) (Scotland) Order 1992 are shown in brackets:

Roof extensions:

No higher than the highest part of the existing roof.

General cases:

Re-roofing and the installation of skylight windows are exempt in general cases;
Dormer windows (extensions) to the roof.

- The roof extension will add less than 50 cu m to the volume of your house;

- The roof extension is to a roof slope that does not face the highway;

- The roof extension does not increase the height of the roof.

Note that if you have previously extended your home, any extra volume created by the dormer extension will have to be added on to the total volume limits relating to extensions. In general cases these are 70 cu m or up to 15 per cent, but reduced to 50 cu m and 10 per cent in special cases. Once these permitted development volumes are used, planning consent will be needed.

Conversion of an existing outbuilding to habitable use, so long as its size and proposal does not lead it to being used as a separate dwelling.

Conversion of existing basements to habitable use, so long as there is no external development proposed.

Conversion of an attached garage to habitable use, if there were no conditions imposed on the dwelling and garage (when built) regarding off-street parking provision; or (in some cases) the dwelling was built before 1 July 1948, when national planning controls were first introduced.

Special cases:
are terraced houses and also properties in the following designated areas: **Area of Outstanding Natural Beauty, National Park, Conservation Area, Norfolk and Suffolk Broads.**

a) The roof extension is no bigger than

25

10% of the existing house (including the roof) in volume or 50 cu m (whichever is the greater), and definitely no bigger than 115 cu m in volume.

b) An extension to the roof, such as a dormer window, is only exempt in the case of terraced houses, if it is no bigger than 40 cu m in volume.

NOTE: In the other special areas listed above, planning consent will be required. In all cases volume is measured externally and includes roof space. There are NO permitted development rights for conversions in or in the grounds of **listed buildings.**

- Cladding the outside of your home is exempt, except within a **Conservation Area, National Park, an Area of Outstanding Natural Beauty, or the Broads.**

- No Article 4 directive is in force on your property, removing Permitted Development rights (they are sometimes used in Conservation Areas or contaminated sites, where greater control is needed).

Designated areas and issues affecting your exemption rights

The planning system allows special areas to be designated where additional controls are needed to keep the place looking special. The most prolific are Conservation Areas, which are defined as 'areas of special architectural or historic interest, the character or appearance of which is desirable to preserve or enhance'. They are identified in the local plan, having been created by the controlling local authority in consultation with parish councils, local amenity societies and the general public. Even if your home isn't a listed building, living in a Conservation Area can invoke similar restrictions on what you do to it.

Another is 'Areas of Special Control' which exist in some parts of the UK, and although they are too small to be considered Conservation Areas, they are designated to protect their architectural or historical value. Your permitted development rights will be affected.

Conversions to council houses will also require the consent of the Local Authority Housing Department. Even recently sold council houses may carry restrictive covenants to this effect.

Farmhouses (properties with agricultural restrictions) are not normally considered as dwellings in respect of these permitted development rights.

The Town and Country Planning Act, which came into being on 1 July 1948, was the first piece of nationwide planning law, and anything built on or after that date in the way of extensions, garages, etc. can potentially be deducted from your permitted development quota. If your property has had any add-ons since 1 July 1948, then you might not have any rights left at all. If this is the case, you may only recover permitted development by demolishing some or all of the old buildings in the same category. It is not unheard of for someone to knock down an old porch, so they can build out a dormer window to a loft conversion without needing planning permission.

In England and Wales, most local planning authorities will notify your neighbours of your proposals, either by letter. Some councils prefer to advertise in the local press or put up a notice nearby, rather than run the risk of leaving someone off the notification list. Neighbours who wish to object have only a couple of weeks to lodge their objections, but it is nonetheless beneficial to notify them of your plans beforehand. In Scotland it is the responsibility of the applicants to consult with their neighbours and submit their signed comments themselves. Forms for this purpose are usually acquired with the planning application forms and should be returned completed when the application is made.

Many people and organisations are consulted in the planning process, parish councils, environmental groups, etc., and it takes some time for all comments to be collected. If there are any objections, it does not necessarily mean that your scheme will be refused. It does, however, usually mean that it will be presented at a planning committee or sub-committee meeting. Most planning authorities operate on the basis that their officers report and recommend the decision to the committee, but effectively the decision is made 'by democracy' in the form of elected councillors rather than by planning officers. You should be entitled to see any such report together with the consultee's comments but you will not be sent them automatically, so make enquiries and ask.

In Northern Ireland, planning applications are made to the Department of the Environment for Northern Ireland who have six divisional offices. These offices carry out the planning function in place of the local authorities, although they do consult with them.

Planning Approval often comes with conditions attached and one is likely to be that work must start within five years if the approval is to remain valid. Another may be that samples of materials (such as a piece of cladding or a roof tile) must be submitted for approval before work starts, or that the exterior materials should match the existing ones on your home.

Refused Planning Consent

Planning authorities must have a good reason for refusing consent. The assumption should by law always be one in favour of an application and not against it – a sort of innocent until proven guilty ethos. But, in the unfortunate event of your application being refused Planning Consent, you should try to establish the exact nature of the objection surrounding it.

The grounds for refusal will be printed on the refusal notice itself, but they are likely to be in planning jargon, so you are going to have to discuss them with your designer or the planning officer who handled the case. It may be that with a few simple amendments they could be overcome and approval given. If this does not seem to be possible, perhaps because there is a fundamental breach of a local planning policy, your only other recourse is to submit a Planning Appeal. Appeals are made to the Office of the Deputy Prime Minister (ODPM) or the Welsh, Scottish Office or DOE for Northern Ireland as appropriate.

Appeals are a lengthy and time-consuming process. Once an appeal is submitted it takes four to five months before the inspector visits the site, and then another two to three months after the visit before a decision is issued. The ODPM do not currently charge for appeals, and so an appeal can be entirely free if you do it yourself – whether you should do it yourself is something else. In practice this only consists of filling out a form, but part of the form is your written statement as to why you consider that the refusal was wrong and should be overturned. This statement needs, if it is to be successful, to contain effective reasons that are judged to be valid points in planning terms. Your personal reasons for needing a second bathroom in the loft with a large dormer window are not relevant issues. The fact that it overlooks only a small part of your neighbour's garden, and only overshadows it for an hour in the morning are.

So getting advice, if not getting an agent to write the report, will help and to this end some engage their solicitor in the task. If they are not fully conversant with local planning policies and ODPM advice circulars (and most won't be), solicitors are likely to be only of administrative help – and expensive administrative help at that. What is really needed is a specialist, somebody *au fait* with planning law and the local policies controlling it in your area. Planning consultants, who specialise in planning applications and appeals, are hence the best choice. Appeals may also be made against conditions of approval, if you consider them to be unacceptable.

You can appeal against the planning authority's failure to give you a decision on your planning application within eight weeks. Not many people do, because it can take the best part of a year to get a planning appeal decided, by which time you might as well have waited for the council to make a decision.

If you do decide to appeal against refusal, you have to lodge the appeal within three months of the refusal date; not just the forms but all the accompanying documents that go with them.

The appeal would normally be dealt with on the basis of a written statement in which you may quote the case for your application to be approved, and request that the council's decision is overturned. Although the written procedure is essentially about preparing a text argument, you can illustrate it with photographs and drawings if they serve a purpose. It's interesting to note that in the Planning Inspectorate's guide booklet, there is a section on what happens if your appeal contains abusive or racist remarks. I imagine they must get a wide variety of objections to planning decisions. Apart from remaining civil during the procedure, you should focus your argument on planning issues and those listed on the grounds for refusal. They will be in code on your refusal notice, as they refer to policies from the local or regional plan. To fight an appeal effectively it helps to know what those coded policies are, and you can visit the planning authority's offices and view them.

Obviously it is important to know what the grounds for refusal were before deciding whether or not to appeal. It may have been refused on a design basis, or it may be a fundamental refusal against the principle of converting the building; either way, you will need to know what it is you are appealing against. Those people who objected to your planning application will be notified regarding the appeal by the local authority, and they will have an opportunity to further comment directly to the Inspectorate, if they wish.

Appeals run to a timetable: after two weeks of receiving your application, the council will send you a questionnaire completed and will notify those who objected before. After six weeks, written reports will be submitted to the Inspectorate by yourself and the local authority, giving your reasons for appealing and theirs for the refusal. The Inspectorate will forward copies to all involved parties, so you don't have to notify them. After nine weeks, you can comment on their report and contest any new issues or points that have been raised that weren't covered before. You then wait for the Inspectorate to notify you of a site visit date. At the visit, you are able to point out features raised in the appeal so that they aren't missed, but you are not permitted to discuss the reason for appealing or argue over the reasons for refusal. If the site can be seen from public land (the road, for example), the inspector may visit unaccompanied.

Planning Inspectors have considerable freedom of judgement in hearing appeals, they get to look at applications holistically and weigh up the views of both the applicants, the local authority and the consultees. They do, however, only make judgement on planning issues. If your objection has more to do with the way the application was processed rather than the decision, then you may wish to complain to the council's complaints officer and ultimately the **Local Authority Ombudsman**. These officials are charged with investigating claims of maladministration if you believe that your application was mishandled and that the correct procedures were not adhered to. Such a complaint will of course take time to be dealt with and may not have any bearing on the decision that was made. In reality few people making planning applications use this procedure in comparison to neighbours who feel their objections have been overlooked and consent still granted. The majority of complaints made to complaints officers and the Ombudsman are rejected as 'no case to answer', since they are grievance-based without evidence of maladministration.

Planning considerations include:

Overshading

If your proposed dormer window is on the south side of a neighbouring building, then the Planning Officer may judge your proposal to be unsatisfactory because of excessive overshading caused by it.

Invasion of privacy

This is a common issue and one that is often raised by neighbours consulted on planning applications. Windows, or worse, balconies that overlook a neighbouring property can be judged to be unacceptable if they create an invasion of privacy, although each case is dealt with on its individual merits. The addition of side windows, in the gable walls of loft conversions or balcony

windows that allow you to step out from the roofline, can fall foul of this issue. With overlooking windows the answer is often to glaze them with obscured glass but sometimes it may be necessary to redesign them as high-level units that have a cill height above most people's eye level, which is normally considered to be 1.78 m.

Design

Nothing could be more subjective than this, but the design of a conversion is a key consideration in planning terms: the shape of the roof, the detail of the fenestration, the type of roof tiles or cladding proposed and so on.

Of course we all know how we want our home to look and having to have our taste judged by some council official can seem like an affront to that right. My only advice is that you sketch out a few different designs in terms of the external appearance and try to weigh them up yourself before submitting your application. If you have the opportunity to run them past your Planning Officer in advance, all well and good. Invariably with conversion work, Planning Officers are looking for subtlety – a design that blends in with and complements the existing home.

Off-street car parking

Garage conversions obviously remove parking space, and how much is available elsewhere on your property is a planning issue. But you may be wondering how a loft or basement conversion can affect your car parking space. Well, unfortunately it can if the conversion contains extra bedrooms.

This is because some planning guidelines cross-reference the number of off-street parking spaces required for a house with the number of bedrooms the house has. For example, a two-bedroom house when built may have needed two car spaces (one on the drive and one in the garage), but a two-bedroom conversion in the loft making the home a four-bedroom property may raise the car parking question and add to the number of parking spaces required.

Check with your local planning department to find out what their ratio of parking spaces to bedrooms is, and whether adding bedrooms to the property will invoke its compliance.

Scale

This is also important and may relate as much to the amount of available room in your roof as to the impact on the neighbourhood. Too big, and the Planning Officer may consider your proposal to be overdevelopment. Raise the roof height above the existing to increase headroom, and that too may be judged out of scale.

In spite of these possible objections and others that may be levied against your application, the majority of planning applications are given consent. The success rate is annually averaged at around the 80% mark for all applications and considerably higher for domestic conversion work.

Alas, the planning system itself is known to be slow, hideously bureaucratic and hopelessly democratic and the eight week 'time limit' that applications are meant to be decided within is frequently extended. The Government is continually criticised over the system and continually claims it is looking at ways to improve it and increase efficiency.

Home office space

If your converted space is to provide you with a home office, you do not need planning consent as a change from dwelling to business use, providing that your home remains principally your home – a place of private residence. It is only a change of use when the majority of the rooms are given over to offices and/or a number of employees work on the premises. Most conversions will only therefore be subjected to the other issues relating to Permitted Development and Planning Consent.

Listed Building Consent

Listed Building Consent is a separate entity. Even where Planning Consent is not required, if you are carrying out conversion work within a listed building, then you will have to seek for Listed Building Consent. If you do require ordinary Planning Consent, a separate application for listed buildings should be made, even though the two will no doubt run concurrently.

Owning a property that is listed has both benefits and drawbacks. On the plus side, the work you do in carrying out the conversion of part of it is zero-rated in VAT, which means that your contractors should not be charging it. They can claim it back from Customs and Excise as part of their annual VAT-return. The other bit of good news is that applications for Listed Building Consent

are free, and no charge is levied by the local authority to process them. The bad news is that the standard required of the design is likely to be much more onerous, as are the controls levied against the proposal in general.

Listed buildings, like Conservation Areas, occur throughout the United Kingdom. Your local planning authority will have a copy of the list for their area should you need to check.

Conversion of an outbuilding that itself is listed or is within the curtilage of a listed building (e.g. your home) attracts such an application, and a considerable amount of design detail may be necessary – large-scale details of the joinery, for example, new or replacement windows and doors. A schedule of the individual members of a timber-framed barn may have to be prepared with drawings indicating each in its position and a note as to its condition. The actual elements themselves should be labelled on-site, providing a reference to this schedule so that if any need to be replaced or repaired through poor condition, they can easily be identified and approval be sought. This will also prove essential if the barn is levelled or damaged by storms during the work. For one thing, the Planning Authority might not let you put it back up without the assurance of knowing what went where.

Building Regulations

The conversion work covered in this book is controlled under the Building Regulations 2000, which basically means you have to submit an application, notify your Building Control Officer for inspections, and comply with the relevant requirements of those regulations. They are written as functional requirements with guidance contained in brochures labelled as Approved Documents, but you can also make reference to British Standards, Euro Codes, Agreement Certificates and other recognised guides for demonstrating compliance.

Because they are updated and expanded quite frequently, it is important for your designer and builder to be up-to-date, but unrealistic to expect them to know all of the implications of requirements or methods of complying. A general knowledge of the current standards should, however, be expected – and the will to ask for advice.

It is unusual (if not actually unheard of) to get from the design submission to the completion certificate of a conversion project without having to consult your Building Control Officer at some point, regarding compliance. Even with approved plans to follow, you may be forced to make changes at some point or another, even if it is due to material availability, and this may have an effect on performance and hence compliance. A simple change in the insulation material, for example, can mean the difference between a completion certificate and non-compliance, so always check with your Building Control Officer.

Some local authorities choose to approve plans with conditions attached, if minor amendments are required, and others will write to your designer agent beforehand to get the plans amended. Whichever way it happens, few applications are 100% approvable on submission, and you need to know what

amendments have occurred or are due to occur to the design before work starts. It is not unusual for these amendments to become lost if a revised plan hasn't been drawn up, particularly as some designers seem happy to leave them for the builder to sort out later. As to whether the builder can sort them out later – or whether indeed it is fair to expect them to – is another matter.

Remember that Building Regulations are legally enforceable rules to ensure primarily that buildings are constructed to protect our health and safety in using them, but they also include energy-efficiency standards aimed at reducing our carbon emissions. The later were increased in April 2002 by quite a large step, making the thermal insulation standards of our homes quite demanding.

Refusal of plans and determinations

Because the requirements of the regulations are functional requirements, there is some scope for deciding what constitutes compliance and what doesn't. The scope is reduced by the Approved Documents which give detailed advice on all the requirements, but they aren't intended to be the sole means of showing compliance. If you feel your designer's work has been unjustly refused approval based on these or any other standards or accepted guides, then you can appeal to the ODPM for a determination. The ODPM will consider both sides of the argument and make an informed decision on which to support – a judgement as a referee, and a legally binding one.

You can only use this procedure at the design stage on refused full plan applications. It is not possible to use it where work is in progress. As with planning appeals, it can be a long long time before the determination is given, so you need to care enough about your design to leave it for a year or so before starting work.

Advice on Building Regulations

Although Chapters 4-6 of this book contain advice that complies with the regulations, the detail of all the requirements is not necessarily given, and given their functional nature you can always benefit from advice unique to your home and your conversion work.

It simply isn't worth your while purchasing all or indeed any of the Approved Documents yourself for a single project. For another thing, they haven't been written for use by the lay person but by professionals within the industry. Not only are they technical documents, but they appear to have been edited by lawyers and are highly cross-referenced and cautiously phrased. In other words, they are virtually impossible to understand.

Your designer and your builder will hopefully be conversant with some of the regulations, but is unreasonable to expect them to be experts in the subject. The only satisfactory way to be advised is by the Building Control Officer who is inspecting the work.

Categories for **exemption** are much fewer and simpler to understand. Currently under the Building Regulations 2000, conversion work is only exempt if it is not classed as 'material alteration or work'. Material

alteration or work is anything that changes the use of the space, for example a garage or a loft space to a room, or anything that affects the structure of the building – so even the boarding out of a loft for storage use could be said to require an application.

In short if the loft, outbuilding or garage has already been **legally** converted in the past and you wish to improve upon it by refurbishment and repair, you may not need to make an application, but otherwise you will. Check with your local authority Building Control Officer for confirmation of exemption before proceeding.

Site inspections

Once work has commenced on the conversion, some inspections will be carried out by the Building Control Officer at various stages. It is a legal requirement for you to notify them, requesting an inspection at these stages, and often the authority may provide notification cards for you to send in.

The vast majority of local Building Control authorities accept telephone requests along with FAX, post or e-mail notification for their intermediate inspections, but still require some form of written notice for commencement and completion of the work. You may wish to contract out the inspection notification to your builder, who should be aware at what stages they are required, but it is worth checking that the notices are being made.

The stages for notification usually include:

1) Commencement – 2 days' notice

2) Foundation excavation - 1 day's notice

3) Foundation concrete -1 day's notice

4) Oversite preparation - 1 day's notice

5) DPC - 1 day's notice

6) Drains before covering - 1 day's notice

7) Drains testing - 1 day's notice

8) Occupation - 1 day's notice

9) Completion - 2 days' notice

With conversion work in particular, additional inspection notices may be required by some authorities, such as exposure of existing foundations, or checking structural timbers and beams before covering them, so check with your Building Control Officer.

Part of the fees payable to Building Control cover the inspection service, as a one-off payment. In a Building Notice submission all the fee is usually paid in advance on deposit of the notice, but otherwise you can expect to be invoiced for the inspection service after the first inspection has been made.

While the Building Control Officer's function is to carry out periodic checks to see if you are meeting - or planning to meet - the requirements of the Building Regulations, they do not supervise the work on your behalf.

You need to engage a surveyor in supervising the work if you wish to monitor the quality of workmanship your builder will apply, since the controls exercised by the regulations do not extend to any standards of workmanship or quality beyond what is necessary for health and safety. As an alternative, a private surveyor can apply some quality control to the work, and can be authorised to make stage payments as appropriate.

Completion certificates

Before your contractors are fully paid up and have left you for their next customer it is vital that you have received a Completion Certificate from your Building Control office. This is a valuable piece of paper which will be required should you sell the property or re-mortgage, and it is only issued once the controlled work is complete and a completion inspection has been made. It is a statement that the work complies with the Building Regulations. Until now, you may only have a Plans Approval notice that confirms your plans comply.

In Scotland, you may have to submit a Certificate of Safety for the electrical installation before you can receive a completion certificate.

What if you or a previous owner have carried out conversion work without getting the necessary consents?

There are procedures for correcting unauthorised work if it wasn't done too many years ago.

Let's deal with **Planning Permission** first. If you've discovered that the conversion should have had Planning Consent and didn't, it is usually a case of making an application retrospectively. If the Planning Authority then decides that the work isn't acceptable and breaches planning controls, they might decide to instigate enforcement action against you, the owner.

Normally this would mean that you would be advised formally of the reasons for refusing it consent and also on what measures you need to take to remedy the breach. They would fix a date by which this corrective work would need to be complete by. It might, for example, be the reduction in height of a dormer window that was overshadowing a neighbouring house.

They may implement this enforcement by way of a condition imposed on your Planning Consent, or they may refuse consent and serve an enforcement notice. Conditions of approvals are enforceable, and if you don't meet them the authority has the power to serve a Breach of Condition notice on you.

As with normal applications, you have the right to appeal against an enforcement notice if you wish to. Until the appeal is decided by the Secretary of State, the notice is suspended and unenforceable.

With regard to a Breach of Condition notice, there is no right of appeal and you run the risk of prosecution if you fail to comply with it. It is, however, possible to apply to the Planning Authority itself to have a condition removed.

For detailed advice on how to appeal against enforcement notices, contact your local Planning Authority or the Planning Inspectorate.

Building Regulations have been in their current format of 'functional requirements' with guidance notes (approved documents) since November 1985, and if the work was done after then, you are eligible to apply for a **Regularisation Certificate**. This is retrospective approval. The fee you pay is slightly more than the standard fee (120 per cent of it), but you do not have to pay VAT on it. Alas, it is usually not as easy as paying a fee and waiting for the certificate to arrive. The Building Control officer will have to inspect the work done, and this could mean exposing parts of the

construction. He or she will want to assess the structural work of the conversion, and you might be required to provide structural calculations and details justifying this element. Weather resistance, insulation and ventilation will also be on the list of things to check out, together with the all important fire safety issues. Whatever the requirements were at the time the work was executed will apply now, and it is quite likely that you will have some corrective or additional work to do to bring the conversion up to scratch. Once this is done and the inspector is happy that the conversion complies, a Regularisation Certificate will be issued, and you should keep this with the property deeds. It will prove invaluable should you ever sell or re-mortgage your home.

Since conversion work is mostly internal, it throws up more unauthorised projects than anything else. Loft and garage conversions illegally done are numerous. Leaving them as unauthorised is not a good idea. For one thing, they may represent a threat to the health and safety of your family and visitors. For another, you will find it difficult, if not impossible, to sell the home or re-mortgage it when you want to.

Other matters of law
Party Wall, Etc. Act 1996

Party walls (or separating walls) are those which divide one property from another in the case of semi-detached or terraced properties. Although the boundary line may run though the middle of such a wall, legally both property owners have rights to the whole wall. This is because they both

rely upon the whole wall for protecting their property from fire and sound transference, so each party needs to know if the other is doing anything to it.

Because it is also possible to undermine the stability of nearby foundations by excavating the ground alongside them, the Act also covers excavation of foundations for underpinning, or indeed anything else that might threaten the foundations.

The Party Wall Act was introduced to England and Wales in general in April 1997, but has existed in London under the London Building (Amendment) Act since 1939. Its aim is to prevent neighbour disputes over party walls ending up in the courts by setting down a procedure for consultation. If London is anything to go by, it seems to work, because only 20 cases out of roughly 2000 end up in court each year.

This Act is an important one for conversion work on semi-detached or terraced homes. It sets out your right to carry out work on the party wall between you and your neighbour that is necessary to facilitate your conversion. For example, you may need to install a beam in your loft conversion and the end bearings may fall on a party wall. The Act accepts your need to do so, but requires you to notify your neighbour, who jointly owns the wall, in a prescribed time.

So you have rights under this Act, but you also have duties. Even when it comes to sitting the end of a beam on the party wall you must notify your neighbour in advance of carrying out the work, and allow them to respond.

There are some minor works, which are exempt, such as plastering the wall,

fixing electrical wiring and sockets to the wall, and generally putting up fixtures and fittings.

What is controlled is any building work that might affect the way in which the wall is loaded, but if you are in any doubt about whether your proposed work requires you to notify the neighbours, seek the advice of a qualified party wall surveyor.

If you forget or overlook the notification procedure, your neighbours are able to seek a court injunction or other legal redress requiring you to stop work.

How do I notify?

This needs to be done in writing, but obviously you should talk to the neighbours as well. The notice should contain your name and address as well as your builder's. It should state that it is being given in accordance with the Party Wall Etc. Act 1996 – its official title – and give full details with plans if appropriate of what you intend to do and when you intend to do it.

If the neighbours rent the place next door, you will also have to send a copy to the landlord, as well as to them as tenants. If the place is empty, you may post the notice on the building somewhere prominent.

As you've probably gathered by now, this law is more about giving notice of your intentions than asking for permission. The notice must be given at least two months beforehand, and any response must come within 14 days. However, if the neighbours don't respond at all or if they respond with objections, surveyors may be needed on both sides to reach an agreement.

Unfortunately, the Act does say that if they haven't responded a 'dispute' has arisen, and so for this reason alone it pays to talk to your neighbours and agree the details informally before serving the notice on them – it isn't meant to be a surprise!

One other benefit of telling them first is that if they agree you don't have to wait for two months before doing the work.

Disputes

OK, so you and your neighbour have a disagreement about the work you are proposing to the party wall. In the first instance you might want to ask your designer, structural engineer or builder if there is any other way of doing it. The chances are that there is another method that your neighbour can live with, and you don't really want to be paying for a party wall surveyor if you can sort it out yourself. For example, that beam that needs to bear 200 mm deep into the wall – it might just be possible to support it on a hangar that is expansion-bolted in place on the surface of the wall, thus avoiding the need to build it in.

If, despite everything, you still can't agree and a surveyor is appointed, their task is to draw up a 'Party wall award' – not a gold statuette of an irate neighbour, but a legally binding agreement of the work that is to take place, on a certain date/s with rights of access to their side if necessary. The award should also record the state of the wall next door, so if there is any claim against damage arising from the proposals it can be fairly assessed.

If your neighbour still does not agree to the award details, they have 14 days to appeal to the County Court objecting. I suppose the biggest hurdle that this Act has to clear is with the neighbour who just refuses to play, doesn't respond, doesn't appoint their own surveyor and so on. Well, you can appoint a surveyor for them so that the procedure goes ahead, but it should not be the same one that you are using. With you being the person benefitting from this work and the one who is proposing to have it done, you have the total bill to pay – you can't share it.

Don't forget that your home may be detached but with linked garages, and the wall between them is likely to be a party wall, so garage conversions as well as loft conversions may come under the same heading.

This Act also has some other elements attached, such as the excavating of trenches near boundaries. Nothing to do with party walls, but if your conversion work means underpinning foundations close to a boundary, the Act applies. 'Close' is defined as 3 m or deeper than their foundations, or 6 m if within a 45-degree splay from the bottom of their foundations. This is about undermining or robbing support from your neighbour's foundations by digging or underpinning your own.

If your proposed underpinning is within 6 m of your neighbour's foundations, you may well have a duty under the Party Wall Act 1996 to notify the owner of that property of your intentions. I say likely because it does depend upon the depth of their foundations in relation to yours. Consider the diagram on page 38 which shows when the Act applies and when it doesn't.

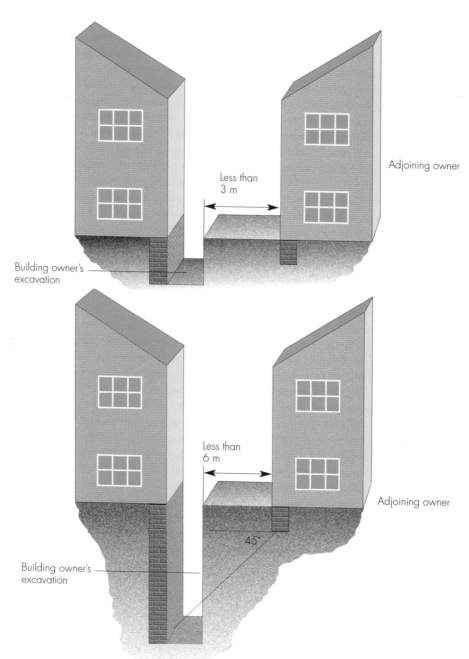

Adjoining owner

Less than
3 m

Building owner's
excavation

Less than
6 m

Adjoining owner

45°

Building owner's
excavation

Excavations controlled under the Party Wall Act 1996.

If your underpinning is to be done on foundations to a boundary wall itself, you can only allow your foundations to cross the boundary by virtue of their design spread after giving one month's notice to the neighbouring owner.

Locating the boundary

We spend a good deal of time on boundary matters as homeowners. Whether they be fences, walls or hedges, the boundaries of our homes are often lost, misunderstood and fought over. The problem is that there is only one source of verification on this subject – and it isn't always very clear. The deeds of your property should show or describe what boundaries exist, and this information is transferred to the HM Land Registry Office, where title deeds and copies of site plans edged in red can be bought.

If you are fighting over inches, then these small-scale maps are not going to help; only a surveyor acting as arbitrator and armed if necessary with a laser theodolite, can tell you precisely where the boundary should be drawn. It is far easier to err on the side of caution and follow the procedures of the Act, even if you are uncertain whether it applies, rather than expend time and money on establishing the exact position of the boundary. As ever, keep your neighbours informed of your proposals.

Wildlife

If you are lucky enough to have a roost of bats in your roof or some other protected species such as barn owls or swallows living in your barn, then you must notify one of two bodies if your conversion works are likely to disturb them. And I would wager that in most cases it would disturb them.

The bodies are: for England – **English Nature** (EN); for Wales – **Countryside Council for Wales** (CCW). They should be able to advise you on how best to avoid upsetting them, or indeed whether the work should go ahead. Both the EN and the CCW have a free booklet entitled *Focus on Bats* which explains the law and gives information on these flying mice.

Health and safety

Health and safety legislation has evolved somewhat in recent years (you might have noticed), and in the building industry, which seems at times to attract people with a circus background, the legislation has been extended to the design as well as the building of projects. Designers have a responsibility under the Construction (Design and Management) Regulations 1994, to minimise the risks associated with building work. They can do this by specifying safe working practice procedures when risks are involved, such as when installing a steel beam in the roof, by detailing the sequence of work and how the beam is to be brought into position.

As the homeowner having domestic building work carried out on your house, you are exempt from the provisions for 'clients' under these regulations and have no responsibilities. Other parts of the CDM Regulations only apply to domestic building work where the house is also used as a business premises. The Health and Safety Executive will be able to give you more information on the latter.

CHAPTER 3

Builders

Finding a builder

I ought really to have named this section 'finding a good builder', because it usually isn't difficult to find a builder in Britain. If we were once a nation of shopkeepers, we now could be a nation of builders. The problem is many of our builders were shopkeepers a week ago, or insurance salesman or window cleaners.

Builders are not, and never have been required to be registered or qualified at what they do, and yet they have the potential to blight or devalue our homes through sheer ignorance, and turn them into dangerous structures through incompetence. The skills shortage in the building industry is acute. Finding skilled tradesmen is not just something that homeowners find difficult, major building contractors struggle to find them too. Accomplished tradesmen are never short of work and never seem to have to advertise; their work finds them, and since their trade can keep them busy

10 Expert Points

HERE ARE TEN EXPERT POINTS TO HELP YOU FIND THE RIGHT BUILDER:

1 SHORTLIST
Prepare a shortlist of four or five builders, including at least two from your local area to avoid extra travelling costs. Get advice from your designer.

2 QUOTES
Invite them to give you a detailed and written quotation for the work (not an estimate) once you have had your plans approved. It will prove difficult, if not impossible, to get anything but a vague estimate without approved plans.

3 DETAIL
Consider how detailed the quotation is. Does it refer to the drawing numbers and details, etc.? Did the builder spend time inspecting the site as well as studying the plans, and does the quotation list out the supply and fit of issues like how many light fittings, power points, radiators and so on— in other words, all the details that are not shown on the plans. Do not leave these issues to be resolved later.

4 TRADE ASSOCIATION
Check to see if they advertise any trade association membership. Do they offer a warranty on their work, and how much will it cost? Do the trade association offer a free arbitration service if you and your builder enter into dispute?

5 PREVIOUS WORK
Request a short list of previous contracts recently completed (within the last 2 years), and once you have received it, select one or two of them and ask if it would be possible to view the work or contact the owners. Most builders are happy to arrange this, if they have satisfied clients.

6 TIME SCALE
With conversion work, your home is likely to be disrupted while it is being carried out. It is important to get some measure of how long a builder takes to complete projects like yours. As well as getting a 'contract time' with the quote, make it clear that if you give them the job, 'time' will be a part of the contract.

on one job for weeks, it is essential to book them in advance.

As with designers, it is wise to find a contractor who has considerable experience in the type of conversion you're proposing. Of course, cowboy builders can claim to be 'specialists' as well, and many find loft conversions easy money. Taking four weeks to partly destroy someone's roof before demanding more money to finish the work is common practice for some rogue traders, who presumably find that people are more willing to pay up when half their roof is missing.

Loft conversions can be quite lucrative to a well-organised contractor who can specialise in them and little else. If they work across a county or region, a well-managed, medium-sized firm of contractors can convert dozens of lofts every year; some may only take them a few weeks from start to finish. Yet one who is simply disorganised can stretch a loft conversion out for several months, adding to the stress of living in a home that is only partially secure and hardly weatherproof.

7 VAT

Some VAT-registered builders may offer a cash price and deduct the tax element, which is not insubstantial. Cash deals are best avoided. They undermine reputable VAT-paying builders, reducing the industry standards and affecting your contractual rights in disputes. The 'cash-deal' builder has still included most of the percentage in his profit margin. For minor conversion works you may be able to find one-man 'contractors' who are not registered, something which doesn't help the builder but does help the customer.

8 INSURANCE

Ask to see evidence of any Public Liability Insurance (which should provide a minimum of £1,000,000 worth of cover). Check that it is valid and not out of date.

9 DEPOSIT-FREE

Avoid builders who request a deposit for materials or whatever up front. Those that need it are unlikely to have the financial security necessary to carry out the work, and may already be refused credit at local builders merchants. Builders with active accounts pay for materials on a monthly credit basis, not on a cash-on-delivery basis and shouldn't require any down payments in advance of starting work.

10 PACKAGE COMPANIES

Some contractors specialising in conversion work, such as loft conversions, offer a design and build, and even design, build and finance package. Be aware of that adage about putting all your eggs in one basket. Their design may be more about making it easier for them to do the work than about your requirements. Their specification may be traded down during the work to save them money. They are more likely to be jacks of all trades than experts of any.

Finally, they have a reputation for being able to convert anything, regardless of the shortcomings of the home (like the lack of headroom for example) without advising the client of those shortcomings. However, they can be extremely quick and well-organised, particularly if they are trading over a large area or nationally. Their labour force will be travelling distances, and they won't want to drag the job out longer than is necessary.

Choosing the wrong builder can not only leave you exposed to the elements and robbed, but it can also convert your home into a dangerous structure.

So how do you find a reputable builder that will do a good job, in good time for a reasonable fee? You could employ your designer to oversee the work as a professional who knows what he is looking at, although this could be costly. Professional Indemnity insurance being what it is, most designers are only covered for design work, leaving only the larger players available for site supervision at a percentage of the contract sum. But you should be able to start drawing up a shortlist of possible builders, with some names from your designer, who ought to know the worst from the best in your area.

Insurance

In addition to checking that your builder is adequately insured, you should also advise your own building insurers of the proposed work. Most buildings insurance policies come with third party cover included, lest a tile from your roof drop onto the head of a passing pedestrian, but they may still require you to pay an extra premium if they consider the risk is increased by the nature of the work. Not notifying them could invalidate your cover.

Legally, without insurance cover you and your builder could be jointly held liable for accidental damage to another person or their property during the conversion. This reflects the fact that as the home-owner you have some responsibility to ensure the person working on your home has taken reasonable steps to protect buildings and people around it, and being insured is part of that responsibility.

Health and safety

Building sites are dangerous places at the best of times, and for a short while your home, or part of it, will become a building site. You will want to ensure that your builder works safely and leaves your home at the end of every day in a safe condition, with beams and structural members properly supported, live wires protected and not left bare, and so on.

Builders at best can have a complacent attitude towards safety, letting it take a back seat to getting the job done, but at worst they can be practically suicidal. Independent tradesmen as self-employed workers, engaged by you, are responsible for their own health and safety and should refuse to work in unsafe conditions, but builders as general contractors employing them have the legal responsibility for their health and safety. This extends to such things as safe scaffolds, ladders, lifting materials and ventilation.

Conversion work is usually tight on space, and it will be necessary for your builder to keep it tidy and free from debris or materials, so encourage them to remove rubbish as they work and only bring in materials as they are needed. The Health and Safety Executive is the controlling authority and has the power to prohibit a builder from working on a site if they are contravening the Construction (Health and Safety) Regulations 1996.

Trade federations, guarantees and quality schemes

Not all builders belong to a trade federation, and indeed there is no requirement for them to. In the past, to be fair, they themselves have not had a good press. One survey revealed that nearly a quarter of all building firms were making false declarations about belonging to them, and it had become quite apparent that they were merely clubs for builders who, having paid the membership fee, were left to trade unregulated. To some extent, they still are, although in recent times they have tried to tighten up their membership criteria and look towards providing some services for their members' customers as well.

If you do check out a trade federation's website or information service, you can expect to receive a list of registered members in your locality and details of some add-on features such as a insurance-backed guarantee or an independent arbitration service. The guarantees are usually available for a small percentage of the contract sum. It says something about the nature of the industry and these bodies when you realise that you are buying specialist insurance at the end of the day and not getting cover by virtue of their membership. Free guarantees are becoming commonplace with top-quality materials where the manufacturers have some confidence that you will not be making a claim, but obviously the same can't be thought about workmanship yet.

Your local authority Building Control department may offer an insurance warranty scheme based on their inspections or may have some liaison with existing trade association schemes.

Warranties are insurance policies like any other. You pay a fee that is often somewhere between 1 and 2 per cent of the contract sum and you are covered for ten years or so against particular misadventures.

You can expect cover against the loss of a deposit paid to the builder or defects due to their bad workmanship or poor materials, although often claims in this instance have to be against failures in the first two years in general. Structural failures are normally covered for the full period of the warranty, as they are unlikely to occur.

You can also expect that if you fall out with your builder in the middle of the job, a refereeing service will be provided and if necessary an alternative builder appointed to finish the work. This would also apply if the builder went bankrupt, died or disappeared into the sunset before completion.

Make sure that the cover extends to sub-contractors or nominated suppliers engaged in the project by your builder. Not many builders complete work these days without using some sub-contracted labour somewhere along the way.

Normally, any insurance warranty covers the property, and if you sell up before the term ends, the cover automatically passes to the new owners.

So although the cost of insurance may not be insignificant, it is a small price to pay for peace of mind in a building industry fraught with problems of disputes and poor workmanship.

Quality Mark

Much thought and effort is being put into cleaning up the industry's poor reputation, and more schemes are springing up all the time. The government itself has, and is still trying to establish a voluntary registration scheme for builders. Developed in partnership with the industry, consumer groups and local authorities, the DTI **Quality Mark** hopes to provide a list of professional firms.

The benefits would include an independent complaints procedure, a warranty (available at cost) and the knowledge that the builder has been audited in respect of his financial probity and work. In time the register would develop, the symbol would be nationally recognizable, duff builders would be booted off it and cowboys would be out-marketed by the government – at least that's the plan. It's been slow to start because builders could see no benefits in it for them, the registration paperwork was too complex and the joining fee too high. Those issues have been addressed, and with the help of local councils, the government's Quality Mark may in time become real.

Quotations and estimates

In inviting any builder to price for your conversion project, you should understand the difference between a quote and an estimate. You may think they are different words for the same thing, but they each have a separate legal meaning.

A **quotation** is a firm price that represents a contract between the parties. As such it is legally binding, so, having agreed a quotation, your builder must stick to it. If they do not and at the end of the job they present you with a larger, unagreed final bill, then in law, you are only obliged to pay the quotation price. The reason most quotes never bear much resemblance to the final bill is because of changes or variations that have occurred along the way, and it is essential that these are agreed, documented and priced as variations to the original quote.

If the quotation does not mention VAT, you may assume (in law) that it is VAT-inclusive, and should your builder add on VAT later to his bill, again you are only obliged to pay the original quotation sum. If a builder is not VAT-registered it is unlikely that he will have the facilities to engage in anything but minor works, since it is his annual turnover that qualifies him for registration. Quotations should contain enough detail of specification or at least refer to the numbered and dated plans for the project as 'contract documents'.

An **estimate**, on the other hand, is a stab in the dark, a best guess, and legally it favours builders to the nth degree, allowing them to present a higher final bill without any warning, since it was not legally binding. The only way a price headed up with the word 'estimate' can become binding is when it is accompanied by a written agreement stating that the price shown is a firm price. If your builder will only provide an estimate, try to agree in writing a 'maximum price' which will not be exceeded and that will serve as a binding agreement.

Contingency sums

Some elements of conversion work may be difficult, if not actually impossible, to price with a fixed sum, and for this reason 'contingency sums' can be included. They will serve to protect both you and the builder from nasty surprises that have a habit of cropping up as soon as work begins. Agree a reasonable figure with builders quoting for the work, and ask them to include it in the quotation. Reasonable could be around 5% of the value of the work for most conversions, for example, 'Allow the contingency sum of £500.00 to be used in agreement only where unforeseen work is necessary or deducted from the final bill'.

Provisional sums

These are similar to contingency sums. The difference is that you know that you are going to be needing them; you simply don't know exactly how much. A provisional sum should be agreed as a round figure which should be enough to cover the actual cost. Once the work is complete and the true cost is known, the adjustments can be made and the part of the sum not used can be deducted from the final bill, for example, 'Allow the provisional sum of £500.00 for relocating the water tanks and associated plumbing'.

Prime cost sums

Prime cost sums, or PC sums as they are usually called, are different to provisional sums only in that they relate purely to the material element of the job and not the labour. They work the same way as provisional sums in that a round figure is agreed that will be sufficient to cover the cost and then the necessary adjustments are made to correct the final bill. Often they relate to elements which the client has yet to decide upon, such as the bathroom tiles, for example, 'Allow the PC sum of £30 per sq m for the supply only of glazed wall tiles to bathroom'.

Variation orders

Very few building projects of any kind make it to the end without some alterations to the original design. Part of the fun of building work is in seeing the project evolve and adding new ideas to enhance it along the way. It simply isn't possible to get all of your wishes down on a sheet of paper before you start, but once you see it taking shape they can spring at you from all directions, and the possibilities of what can be and what can't be achieved are much easier to see. There will inevitably be variations that need to be written down, priced and agreed.

You may only have a legal obligation to pay for the ones you've agreed to, but you will want to be fair with your builder. Many builders make a point of telling you that extra work is necessary as they come to it, and seek your verbal agreement to carry it out and get on with the job. Resist the pressure to make instant decisions, and instead ask them to price for the extra work on a written format.

Written adjustments are often referred to as VOs or variation orders, since in larger projects they are drafted by inspecting surveyors or architects as written instructions from the client to the builder, authorising him to carry out additional work or omit work that was previously agreed. Some trade associations provide standard forms for variation orders to be written on, but you can equally create your own. It is worth doing this, even when there is no cost implication involved, so that disputes are avoided later. A book of variation orders can be kept and jointly signed by both parties against the description of the work and the cost implication. A copy should be kept by both parties, so a duplicate type notebook with numbered pages is ideal for this purpose.

If this system is diligently followed, there are rarely differences of opinion later on. If you cannot agree upon a fixed amount for such a variation because it is unquantifiable by its nature - for example, it involves investigation of concealed wiring or something else that is hidden - you might wish to agree a **daywork rate**.

Daywork rate

This is defined as an hourly labour rate, so you must be careful to monitor the time spent on it. The best way is to maintain a daywork sheet jointly which you can both sign at the end of each day. The hourly rate should be agreed beforehand, and the cost of materials and plant hire will be added to this labour charge along with overheads and profit, if your builder is not able or willing to 'build' the latter into his hourly charge. Daywork is usually costly unless it is reserved for minor work which can be completed in a few hours or, at most, a couple of days.

Contracts

Do not be tempted to settle for a verbal agreement; a gentlemen's handshake may be noble, but it does not stand up to much. You can still purvey an air of confidence and trust even when using a written agreement that both parties sign up to. Some of the friendliest builders I know are also the worst.

Where you are employing an architect or surveyor to oversee the work they will be able to advise you on the most suitable form of contract; indeed, they may recommend using a standard form issued by their own professional institute.

Some builders and tradesmen will have their own forms of contract which they may invite you to sign. Do not be pressurised into signing them until you are ready. Read them carefully first; make sure you understand what the clauses mean and the significance of each of them.

If you feel it necessary to delete, add or amend any parts of the contract, discuss them with the contractor first. Remember that in most cases there will be scope for negotiation over the conditions of the contract, even if the price remains fixed.

Have a look at the details of the contract for small building works on page 50, and see how it compares to the one you are being invited to sign. Trade associations have produced their own standard form contracts for domestic building work like conversions, and these are usually clear, concise and fair to both client and builder - some even have awards from the Plain English Campaign.

Example Invitation to Tender/Letter of Agreement

<name and address of contractor>

Dear............

Ref: ....*<title description of job>*

You are invited to submit a firm quotation for the above.

The work comprises
the...
....and shall include for
incidental works necessary to complete the work to my reasonable satisfaction.

Although a formal contract will not be entered into, the JCT Agreement for Minor Building
Works 1980 Edition (revised 1991 and inclusive of all amendments to date) will be
deemed to apply in the event of any dispute.

Damages for non-completion; liquidated damages will be at the rate of £........ per day/per
week during which the works remain uncompleted.

An amount equal to 2.5% of the total value of the work will be retained for a period
of.........weeks/months after the date of practical completion.

Where applicable, all work is to comply with BS: 8000, Codes of Practice and other British
Standards, material manufacturers recommendations and instructions appropriate to
achieve a satisfactory performance.

The Contractor is to inspect the site of the work prior to submission of the quotation. No
subsequent claim arising from failure to do so will be entertained. All costs incurred in
preparing the tender shall be borne by the contractor.

Include in your quotation the provisional Sum of .... For contingent or unforeseen
works as identified in the schedule of works.

This sum to be deducted in whole or part as agreed by both parties if not required.

The works are to commence on ....and be completed
by.................................

The specification shall be fully priced and a pricing summary sheet duly completed,
signed and dated with the company address. The completed quotation should be sent to:

<your name and address>

and must be received not later than.................*<date required>*

Yours faithfully,

....

Enclosed: Schedule of Work

For small works without professional supervision, you may wish to use a simple letter of agreement like the one shown on page 47, which can also be used as an invitation to tender (quote) for the work.

Invitation to tender/letter of agreement

This can be used for the smallest of projects as both a letter of invitation to tender and agreement document. It requires the parties to defer to the comprehensive standard form issued by the JCT, only in the event of a dispute. This type of letter is often used by larger organisations engaging tradesmen in small jobs on a regular basis, but there is no reason why it couldn't be used for domestic home improvements.

The Contract for Domestic Building Works

This can be used for projects where specific conditions need to be addressed. It covers most of the clauses contained in approved standard forms, but does so more concisely. Sometimes there are particular issues that cause friction during building works that could have been avoided by adding specific conditions to the contract like the:

- Hours of working

- Access to facilities in the house: bathroom, telephone, water and electricity

- Protection of driveways and plants

- Use of radios/music players

- Lighting of fires to burn waste materials, removal of waste materials from site on a regular basis, etc.

Remember that specific conditions such as these may help to relieve the disruption arising from the work, but the conditions must be reasonable and practicable, and some disruption is inevitable if the work is to proceed.

Of course any written agreement is between you and your builder, and you can write one out yourself if you prefer.

Workmanship standards

By far the biggest complaint of those employing builders is workmanship. As a lay person you may not know whether the roof has been correctly constructed or not and will need to rely upon the professionals to check it over. But you will be able to tell when a wall has been badly plastered, when windows haven't been correctly fitted or a door isn't hung right.

It is usually at the end of the contract, when the finishings are somewhat lacking in standard, that the customer realises his builder isn't as skilled as he thought he was. Structural work can be quite forgiving, although if you know what to look for, you will soon be able to spot quality from the rest. With carpentry, for example, it is accurately cut timbers with joints that fit neatly together without gaps showing, equally spaced and well formed; nailing or bolting that hasn't split or butchered the wood but

BS:8000

Part 1	1989	Code of Practice for excavation and filling
Part 2	1990	Code of Practice for concrete work
Part 3	1989	Code of Practice for masonry
Part 4	1989	Code of Practice for waterproofing
Part 5	1990	Code of Practice for carpentry, joinery and general fixings
Part 6	1990	Code of Practice for slating and tiling of roofs and claddings
Part 7	1990	Code of Practice for glazing
Part 8	1989	Code of Practice for plasterboard partitions and dry-lining
Part 9	1989	Code of Practice for cement sand floor screeds and concrete floor toppings
Part 10	1989	Code of Practice for plastering and rendering
Part 11	1989/1990	Code of Practice for wall and floor tiling
Part 12	1989	Code of Practice for decorative wall coverings and painting
Part 13	1989	Code of Practice for above-ground drainage and sanitary appliances
Part 14	1989	Code of Practice for below-ground drainage
Part 15	1990	Code of Practice for hot and cold water services (domestic scale)

Electrical installations should be conditioned as 'installed in accordance with IEE (Institute of Electrical Engineers) Wiring Regulations'.

Example Form of Contract for Domestic Building Works

This agreement between...

<your name>.................................
of...........<your address>........................
....
(Hereinafter referred to as 'the employer')

And

....................................<contractors name>
of..............................<contractors address>
(hereinafter referred to as 'the contractor')

is made on the ————day of—— 20—

Whereas
1. The employer requires the following conversion work to be carried out to convert the
....to
....

And has caused

Drawings numbered.............................

and/or specification dated.................
and/or schedules dated......................
and/or structural design calculations and details dated.............................

(hereinafter referred to with the conditions annexed as 'the contract documents')

showing and describing the work to be done and which are attached to this agreement

2.The contractor has stated in his quotation the sum required for carrying out the work (the sum as stated in article two of this agreement)

3.The contract documents have been signed by both parties.

4.CONDITIONS (hereinbefore referred to)

(I) Standards
The contractor shall diligently and professionally carry out the complete works as detailed within the contract documents in compliance with the applied Building Regulations, using approved materials and workmanship standards to BS: 8000, and with electrical installations installed in accordance with the IEE (Institute of Electrical Engineers) Wiring Regulations.

(II) Duration
The works may start on................................And shall be completed by.............................

Or may be extended to a later specified date by agreement of both parties, or a reasonable extended date for reasons beyond the control of the contractor such as adverse weather.

If the works are not completed by the completion date then the contractor shall pay or allow for, in liquidated damages to the employer at the rate of

£ ......per week

between the contracted date of completion and the actual date of practical completion. The Employer may deduct such liquidated damages from any monies due under this contract.

(III) Defects
Any defects or faults including excessive shrinkage which appear within three months of practical completion due to materials or workmanship shall be rectified and made good by the contractor at his own expense.

(IV) Variations
If any amendments or variations are required by the employer, written instructions shall be given by him within two days of the oral instruction and the price agreed for it before works are carried out. Any inconsistencies or errors in the contract documents shall be corrected and treated as a variation.

(V) Payments
Interim payments shall be made for works carried out and materials brought on to the site at intervals of not less than four weeks. The Employer will pay to the Contractor any fair amount so specified in this respect, within 14 days of the date of invoice.

Retention of.......% (not exceeding 5%) may be deducted from the final payment at practical completion to be released in two halves. The first half at 14 days after practical completion and the second half at 3 months after practical completion.

(VI) Quotation
The quotation shall be a fixed price that shall not take any account of changes to the cost of labour, materials, plant or other resources needed by the contractor to carry out the work.

(VIII) Legal Requirements and Notices
The contractor shall comply with all notices and requirements required by statute, statutory instruments, rules, regulations and bylaws. Including all necessary Notices for inspection to the Building Control Officer. If in complying with these matters of law additional works are necessary that are not shown on the contract documents he shall notify the employer immediately.

(IX) VAT
VAT shall be added to the contract sum where applicable and where it is not separately shown, the sum shall be taken as exclusive of VAT (value added tax)

(X). Insurance
The contractor shall indemnify the employer against any liability, loss, expense, claim or proceedings in respect of personal injury or death of any person, arising from the work. He shall maintain an appropriate level of insurance under the Employers Liability (Compulsory Insurance) Act 1969 as amended. The contractor shall produce evidence as required in respect of his insurance for the employer.

(XI) Determination
by the employer
Should the contractor without reasonable cause default by failing to proceed diligently or suspending the works substantially, the employer may give notice of....... days to him allowing for the default to end. A notice of determination may then be served by the employer on the contractor. If the Contractor becomes bankrupt has a professional liquidator appointed or winding-up order made the Employer may by notice determine the employment of the contractor immediately.

by the contractor
If the employer fails to pay any interim

payments or final payment within the specified time periods or pay any VAT due on the amount, or if the employer unreasonably interrupts or disrupts the execution of the work or suspends the work for at least one month then the contractor may give notice of..........days to the employer, allowing for the default to end. A notice of determination may then be served on the Employer by the contractor.

(XII) Settling Disputes
When either party requires a dispute to be settled, they shall give written notice to the other, of the appointment of an arbitrator. The arbitration shall be conducted in accordance with the Joint Contracts Tribunal Arbitration Rules as amended.

NOW IT IS HEREBY AGREED

Article 1
For the consideration here in after stated the contractor will in accordance with the contract documents attached carry out and complete the work referred to, together with any changes or variations made in accordance with this contract.

Article 2.
The Employer will pay the contractor the sum of ....
For the works, exclusive of VAT

AS WITNESS

The signatures of the parties

the employer ....

the contractor..........................

in the presence of ...(witness)................

name in print...................

address...................... ....

soundly jointed it; joists and rafters that are level and straight.

Workmanship and the difference in the quality of it is highly variable from one tradesman to the next, but obviously there are minimums – bottom lines where the standard is too low to be acceptable. Unfortunately these minimums are not really covered by the Building Regulations, since any judgement of quality is bound to involve cost and the regulations are only seeking to provide health and safety measures with energy conservation thrown in. Having said that, it is possible for work to be carried out so badly that it doesn't meet the requirements of the regulations. A roof may be so badly tiled that the rain comes in, a ceiling so badly plastered that it is unable to resist fire.

In most of these cases the standard of workmanship will have sunk well below the point where you would want the builder to stop work and leave, and so controlling the standard to your own requirements is something you must aim for yourself. If you are unhappy with the quality of the work you must stop the builders at your earliest opportunity and draw their attention to the fact. There is no point in letting the whole job be completed if the standard is lower than your expectations. The British Standards Institute has published a series of standards for each trade on the subject, and these should be stated in the contract documents.

Electrical installations should be installed in accordance with IEE (Institute of Electrical Engineers) Wiring Regulations, and certificates of compliance should be sought from a qualified electrician once the installation is complete. These regulations are again codes of practice rather than statutes, but if you refer to them within your contract or agreement, they will become enforceable under civil law.

Generally electricians are either members of the ECA (Electrical Contractors Association) or the IEE, although there is no legal requirement for them to belong to either. However, any electrical contractor should provide you with a certificate of minor works under BS:7671 for alterations to circuits involved with your conversion.

Quality assurance is still popular, although thankfully it seems to be on the wane. Whether you have seen those signs in garages that spell out their promise to customers or those plaques on the walls that you can look at while you're waiting for the third time to have your exhaust fixed on properly, you'll know that quality assurance is about image. It can be and often is meaningless, but image is still what matters at present, and if you can attain a standard repeatedly, any standard at all, you can be measured and audited by it to receive quality accreditation. It doesn't mean the service you provide is better than any other builder's, it simply means you can deliver it over and over again.

BS:5750 Part 1 is the same standard as ISO:9001, and BS:5750 Part 2 is the same standard as ISO:9002. Now there is a year 2000 edition. They are about systems and not about quality of work and so you don't find many builders brandishing them, but you might come across them with materials, professionals and statutory services who are now competing in the image-is-everything private sector.

Payment

You should always establish the terms of payment. Most contractors will provide this for you, even if you don't, so check their conditions and make sure you are happy with them. The Construction Act 1996 (aka Housing Grants, Construction and Regeneration Act 1996) does not apply to work on home conversions where the client is defined as a 'residential occupier'. Nevertheless, the code it invokes on matters of payment could be of use to you. Bear the following in mind when paying contractors:

- Agree the terms of payment within the contract or agreement.

- It should be specified how much is to be paid and when it is to be paid, the latter being best described as a stage in the works, rather than a time which might not be achieved.

- If, as the owner, you intend to withhold payment due to problems with the workmanship or materials used, then you should notify the builder immediately in writing of the amount you are withholding and the reasons why.

- If you fail to do this but still withhold payment, the builder may give you no less than seven days'

notice of his intention to stop work. The builder's right to stop work ceases once payment is made. The final completion date should be extended to make up for lost time.

- In the case of most conversion work, stage payments arranged at certain stages would be appropriate (e.g. all structural work complete, electrical and plumbing first fix complete).

- The final payment is due within 30 days of practical completion.

- All payments should be made within 17 days of the date they are due (i.e. the billing date).

- By far the best method of payment is the credit card because the Credit Protection Act gives you some protection, particularly in the case of deposits should your builder go out of business before starting.

- If your builder doesn't belong to a credit card scheme, then you might ask for a deposit indemnity. In the case of a limited company, the directors should be able to provide it, and if it isn't limited then the proprietor should. Of course, you must remember that the indemnities will only work if you can locate the people personally afterwards, and this may not be easy if the firm has gone bust.

- Never provide payments in advance of work being done.

Credit agreements

Whether you are paying by credit card or by loan, including those in which the builder is acting as the broker as some package firms do, then you have rights under the Consumer Credit Act 1974. These rights extend to changing your mind shortly after signing, if :

- The credit loan is between £50 and £15,000 and isn't secured by your home.

- You signed the credit agreement after discussing the details face to face with the builder.

- You signed at home or anywhere other than the builder's offices or premises.

You should have been given a copy of the agreement which sets out your rights to cancel it, and you should receive a second copy in the post at a later stage. Be warned, however, that the time limits in which to do so are quite tight.

Other benefits of builder credit finance include extra protection measures against the builder where he is in breach of contract or misrepresentation. This still applies even if the builder is acting as the broker, and means that the lender is equally liable for any claim you have against the builder in these respects. Even if the builders go bust before they starts the job, taking your deposit with them, you will have redress here. The contract sum needs to fall between £100 and £30,000, so this should include most domestic conversion work.

Contract time

Along with payment terms, it is important to include the contract time within your agreement. Your home is to be made at least in part into a building site, and you are going to want it that way for as little time as possible. You might think that builders would be keen to crack on with the job and move on to the next one, and some are. Others, and I'm thinking of those with less work and even less reputation, may want to drag it out and drag as much money out of you as they can along the way. By agreeing on a completion time and invoking a penalty clause for not achieving it, you are giving yourself some peace of mind that you won't fall into the hands of the latter.

You will need to ensure that your builder has access to the site at all times if he is to complete the work to schedule. Locking up and going off on holiday in the middle of the job is likely to lead to your builder finding alternative work which may not fit in with your return. Penalty clauses for delays can work in both ways: if you, the client, have delayed the work, the builder can claim against you.

Snagging

Snagging is the term given to all those bits that need sorting out at the end of the job, like doors that need easing or self-closers adjusting. Ideally, you should review the work with the builder once it is complete, and point out anything that needs attention.

A list should be drawn up and a copy kept by both parties, and here is the important bit – it should not be added to. Snagging lists are meant to be the final word. Builders need to know when they are finished and cannot be reasonably expected to keep returning to jobs *ad infinitum*.

The work is then carried out, and final payment can be made once you are completely satisfied, and once you are sure that the Building Control Officer is also completely satisfied and you are holding a copy of the Building Regulations Completion Certificate. Under no circumstances should you consider the job is complete until this certificate has been issued.

If the contractor is providing you with a guarantee through his trade association, then make sure you have it signed and keep it along with the Completion Certificate before releasing the final payment.

Disputes

If you have a written agreement or contract with your builder and have maintained written variations throughout the job, you will have significantly reduced the risk of getting into a dispute. But building work by its nature can lead to problems, and disputes can arise in spite of all the best intentions. The important thing is to resolve them before they escalate – disputes that are left to fester usually grow until they reach a head, often with the builder leaving the work unfinished and claiming materials back on his way out of the door.

It is always best to agree within the contract who will act as an independent arbitrator if things get to that stage. Often a trade body or a surveyor will serve in this capacity.

Building Control Officers are not available for this purpose, although they can of course regulate over matters of compliance with the work under the Building Regulations, and in this respect their word is final. In cases where a dispute has arisen over the work itself, it will be necessary to have them inspect it and confirm its compliance or detail contraventions.

Whilst the Officer may be called upon as an expert witness to verify these in court, should it come to that, you are far better off engaging your own surveyor to document and photograph the work in preparing your claim. Their agency is likely to serve you better since it should extend to quality of workmanship and contractual matters between you and the builder.

Generally speaking, by the time such matters reach court, both parties have lost, and it is far better to keep the channels of communication open to resolve matters. Site meetings to jointly view and discuss problems, perhaps with the surveyor or Building Control Officer present, are a good start. It may be possible to agree different ways in which the work can be rectified to the satisfaction of both parties.

It should go without saying that you should strive to adopt a civil but business-like manner through all your dealings, and make sure you maintain good records until the dispute is resolved – one way or another.

If you have to engage another contractor to complete the work, you may wish to make a claim to the County Courts to recover the loss. If the amount that you are claiming is less than £3,000 (£750 in Scotland) you can take your builder to the County Court under the Small Claims Procedure. In 2002 the County Courts introduced an Internet service that allows small claims to be made on-line, such is the demand for their services.

Finance

Borrowing money for home improvements doesn't usually prove too difficult, but you should consider the benefits and drawbacks of different types of loans or credit before signing on the dotted line.

Credit cards may well be the favoured way of making payments, but only if you settle the bill monthly and thus avoid high interest rates. Shop around for loans and see how the different banks and building societies compare with the products they offer and the rates they charge. Essentially there are only two types of loan – secured and unsecured.

Secured loans

These use your home as security against you defaulting on the payments. The terms for these are more favourable, since the risk for the lender has been reduced. The loans can be extensions to your existing mortgage over the same period of time.

One of the consequences of secured loans is the need to have your property independently valued, since your lenders will need to know whether the amount you're borrowing will be covered by the value of the property. Home conversion work should add value to your home, and this will need to be included in the valuation.

Secured loans must be presented with the prerequisite statement about the consequences of defaulting on the loan – in other words, the bit that says your home is at risk if you do not meet the repayments. This security allows them to offer you the money at a reduced interest rate than to that of an unsecured loan and hence you benefit. Before it is released the lender may require sight of your plans and approval notices, to ensure that your proposals are lawful.

The loan can usually be repaid over a period of up to 25 years, but there is normally a minimum borrowing amount set and a maximum that is somewhere near to the value of your home. Most banks and building societies offer personal loans that are secured in the same way, and without fail insurance is sold (usually hard-sold by employees on performance pay) if you wish to protect yourself against not being able to meet payments, due to sickness or redundancy.

Unsecured loans

These may be more suitable for smaller advances, where repayment will often be over a shorter period of up to 10 years, but frequently less. Interest rates are higher because your home is not available as security. These loans can be more flexible as a result, allowing you to pay off larger amounts to reduce the term, for example. You won't carry the risk of losing your home should you default on it, but you will have to pay a bit more in interest.

Remortgage

Financing home improvements by re-mortgaging has become popular over the last decade. Lenders have had to compete fiercely to steal each other's customers and persuade people to re-mortgage with them.

Financial cash incentives of up to several thousand pounds have been on offer to entice new customers, along with reduced or fixed-rate interest terms but, as with any type of 'too good to be true' deal, there are nearly always clauses in the small print. Many of the offers tie you in to buying their buildings insurance or prevent you from moving again without incurring high management charges.

These offers never seem to be available to the existing borrower, and hence only by moving your mortgage to another company can you take advantage of them, but always investigate the full nature of their terms. Banks and building societies are quite capable of behaving unscrupulously in selling their products, and do not always trouble themselves with personally explaining the conditions of their loans.

Grants

The rules for the qualification and awarding of grants change quite often and are subject to the political and economic climate of the time. The current system is administered on a discretionary basis by each authority, and it is worth making a speculative phone call to their grants section before you proceed too far. You will only stand a chance of getting a home improvement grant for a conversion if:

- Your property is less than ten years old.

- Your property already meets the fitness standard and has the basic amenities – toilet, shower or bath, kitchen, etc.

- A cheaper way of providing the amenities, such as converting an existing bedroom into a bathroom, can be found.

- If you are a council tenant (except in the case of disabled facilities grants – see below).

- If you just want to increase your living space, e.g. with a bedroom or lounge conversion.

- If the property is a second home or holiday cottage.

- If you haven't been an owner or occupier for at least three years.

By far the most commonly awarded grants for conversions come from the adaptation of existing bedrooms or spaces to provide bathroom facilities that were previously lacking. With successful applications the amount of grant aid you will receive may be determined by a means test, an income and expenditure analysis that reveals your disposable income. This is to ensure that the most help goes to those who are least able to pay for it themselves. Your local authority will give you some advice on how means testing is carried out and advise you on

how much, if anything at all, you will have to contribute yourself to the cost of the project.

Grants are usually awarded with conditions attached, e.g.:

- The work must be completed within 12 months.

- You must not change the contractor whose estimate was accepted.

- You must live in the property for a minimum of five years after the work is complete.

If you fail to meet these conditions, the authority can require you to repay the grant aid.

House renovation grants

Although this type of grant is mainly available for essential repair work, it could be available to carry out a conversion if it is needed to bring the house up to the 'fitness standard.' If, for example, the property was very old and lacked the basic amenities of an indoor bathroom or toilet, the conversion of the loft to provide these facilities might be grant-aidable. The fees for the design work and those payable to the council for planning and building control may be included within the grant aid.

Disabled facilities grants

If you are registered disabled and your conversion is sought to provide special facilities for you. Perhaps it is the conversion of your garage to a ground floor bedroom or a shower room with a flush floor shower, then you may well be eligible for a disabled persons grant.

Once again these grants are administered by the local authority, but often they involve occupational therapists from the health authority who may help in deciding what facilities should be provided. Most authorities have agencies for dealing with disability grants – these are usually labelled as 'Home Improvement Agencies' and they exist to help the elderly and disabled in the community. They can offer an advisory and design service in addition to administering the grant aid and dealing with the builders. They will also submit applications for building regulations and planning approval, the fees for which are usually exempted for disabled facilities.

Home-insulation and energy-efficiency grants

Home Insulation Grants are only available for existing homes that require additional insulation and to those qualifying homeowners. They can not be applied for in the case of new conversion work where the insulation must be built in as work proceeds even if you qualify as an eligible applicant.

If you are planning on changing your boiler to a more energy efficient one, you may qualify for a grant from the Energy Saving Trust. They were set up by the government after the 1992 Rio Earth summit to help promote energy efficiency and reduce carbon emissions. To this aim grants are available for a variety of energy saving installations. Phone them or check their website for details (see Useful Contacts).

CHAPTER 4

Lofts

The high life

If you are looking to create additional living space but are reluctant to lose valuable garden space, then a loft conversion could be the answer. Rooms in the roof make for attractive living space and are becoming increasingly popular. With sloping ceilings and skylight windows, loft rooms can enhance your home by creating different and interesting areas in which to work and live. Often they do not require planning permission, and for most people it will prove significantly cheaper to convert the attic space into an extra storey of living accommodation than to build outwards at ground level with an extension – but there are drawbacks as well as benefits.

The conversion will have to comply with the Building Regulations to ensure that it will provide you with a safe environment – the two principal issues and regulations, that control the design of loft conversions are structural stability and fire safety. Even if you only intend to convert your attic to an occasional hobby room, you should consider what all the implications on the structure are likely to be.

Ten FAQs on loft conversions

1. Are the joists in my loft strong enough to be a floor?

What were previously ceiling joists will become floor joists, and as such the weight increase may be up to four times greater. Ceiling joists are invariably only 100 mm deep and will need to be strengthened in the early stages of a conversion. The most common way to do this is to install new deeper joists alongside them, which are capable of carrying the new floor deck. It is not a good idea to try enlarging the existing joists by nailing additional sections on top of them.

2. Will the rafters be strong enough once the struts and supports are removed?

In conventional designs a short timber stud wall, known as 'ashlaring', is built perhaps 1 m in from the wall plate to help support the rafters. This ashlaring will replace any diagonal struts in the attic, which can then be safely removed. It is worth asking your structural engineer to design the floor joists so that they will also support the ashlaring, as this is the most cost-effective option. If this isn't possible the alternative is to install beams of either steel or timber from which to build it. Builders often dislike using steel beams in attics where access is difficult and working space tight, but if RSJs are to be used it may be necessary to deliver them in manageable sections with end plates that will allow them to be joined together when they are in position. As a compromise between timber and steel beams, flitch beams are ideal, as they comprise two sections of timber bolted alongside each other and a mild steel plate sandwiched in between.

3. Does my roof lend itself to an attic conversion?

This is a tough question to ask yourself

– it ranks alongside 'Does my bum look big in this?' and equates to the same thing. Not all lofts are convertible, and trying to force one to fit where clearly it doesn't is not wise.

If your home was built prior to the mid-1960s then your roof will be of a traditional cut-and-pitch construction, perhaps of 100 mm-deep rafters and joists with a purlin supported by a few diagonal struts. Measure the vertical height from the ridge at the apex of the roof down to the joists, and if you have 2.3 m or – preferably – more available, you have the ingredients for an excellent loft conversion.

Properties built after this time may well have used trussed rafters to construct the roof, and although it is still possible to convert the attic the process is more complicated.

It is quite possible for your property to become a dangerous structure if the proper sequence of construction isn't followed. The web of diagonal struts must not be cut out until the new floor and roof supports are in place to take the load. A 'sequence of work' should be drawn up by your design engineer that identifies the order in which the structural work must take place, allowing the conversion to proceed safely. As trussed rafter members are invariably smaller in size than traditional roof timbers, it is common practice that more support beams will be needed to reduce the spans – the truss rafters that carry the roof tiles or slates may only be capable of spanning 1.5 m, for example. And since trussed rafters are used to span roofs up to 10 m across, several new purlins may be needed to help support them at regular centres. The situation is exacerbated by the fact that the trusses are spaced further apart than the timbers in a cut roof.

4. Do I need to go to a specialist loft conversion company?
Specialist loft conversion companies that offer a design-and-construct package should be familiar with the laws and regulations governing them, and are usually capable of carrying out the works expediently. In the case of nationwide companies, the labour they use will be in local lodgings for the duration of the work, and they will be keen to finish the job in a fixed time.

These companies have the benefit of being well-organised, but seldom appreciate changes to the design or unforeseen problems that may arise, and most will sell you a loft conversion of any size, regardless of how little space you will actually gain from it. The sales pitch invariably runs along the lines of a third of your house being empty space just waiting to be occupied. When you think in terms of floor area this seems plausible, but when you consider how much of that floor area you will comfortably be able to walk around in, the fraction will drop to nearer one-sixth.

5. Will there be enough headroom?
Looking at the floor layout plans for your new loft isn't going to help unless they have been overmarked to indicate where the line of comfortable ceiling height stops and the slope of the roof takes over. Remember that not only will

you be unable to stand upright in some areas, you won't be able to stand a wardrobe in places either, so ask about headroom and look at the cross-section depicted on the plans to appreciate just how much usable floor area you will be gaining. Floor layout plans of loft conversions always look deceptively large, but remember that ashlare walls are only 0.7 or 1 m high. Find out where the full headroom stops, and ensure that that line is marked on the plan.

Be sure on how much headroom you will want to feel comfortable in the loft room before going ahead. Some companies will sell you an attic conversion regardless of ceiling height. 2.3 m is the standard height for normal rooms, and although you may not have this available in the roof, make sure that it isn't too much lower. The end result could prove claustrophobic, as well as making obstacles out of light fittings. On a staircase and its landings the minimum safe headroom is considered as 1.9 to 2 metres.

It follows that given the pitch of the roof and its span, the maximum headroom is known and for roofs of a 30° pitch, a roof will need a span of 8 or 9 m to reach enough height at the ridge to make it convertible, whereas a roof of 45° pitch will make it with a span of just 5 or 6 m.

The table below of roof pitches and spans will give you some idea of whether sufficient headroom will be available. Note that:

● Spans are measured between the wall plates.

● Approximately 400 mm has been taken off the height to allow for floor joists, ridge beam and finishings.

● The heights given are maximum ceiling heights available beneath the ridge (apex of the roof). No allowance has been made for raised collar ties.

6. What sort of windows should I have?

Because of headroom problems dormer windows are often favoured over skylights that lie flat to the roof slope.

ROOF PITCH	ROOF SPAN				
	5 m	6 m	7 m	8 m	9 m
30°	-	-	-	1.9 m	2.1 m
35°	-	-	2 m	2.4 m	2.6 m
40°	-	2.1 m	2.5 m	2.9 m	-
45°	2 m	2.5 m	3 m	-	-
50°	2.5 m	3 m	-	-	-

They allow the full ceiling height available to be extended out to the window face. If you do choose dormers in your design, be aware that you might need planning consent, and consider whether your roof has sufficient height to allow them to have small pitched roofs, or whether you will need them to have flat roofs. Increasing the height of your roof to convert the loft will mean not only applying for planning permission, but also a lot of extra building work.

If correctly proportioned, dormers can make attractive features externally as well as increasing space inside, but if you live in a conservation area or a listed building, it may prove difficult to acquire planning consent for them. Skylights, on the other hand, do not require planning permission because they do not alter the shape of the roof. Locating one on the south-facing slope of your roof, however, will mean providing it with a blind, as loft rooms are always the warmest room in the house, even without the sun to heat them directly.

For those windows that are out of reach a range of accessories are available, such as electrically operated blinds. It is also worth ensuring that your window has a 'crack vent' position or 'trickle vent' fitted that allows some air to enter even when the window is locked and secure. In addition, special designs that can be used for fire escape exits, and others made specifically for Conservation Areas, are available from manufacturers. More information on windows can be found further on in this chapter.

7. Where should the stairs be positioned?

One of the most important elements of a loft room design is the positioning of the stairs, since it is the one factor that could both save you space and save your life. Fire safety is an important issue when you're creating a third floor

Look towards achieving continuous stairways

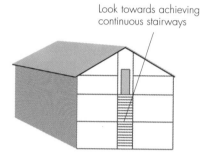

Option 1: fire door at loft room

Extend first-floor landing to enclose stairs

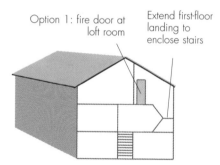

Option 2: fire door to loft stairs on first floor

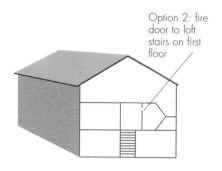

Stair positioning.

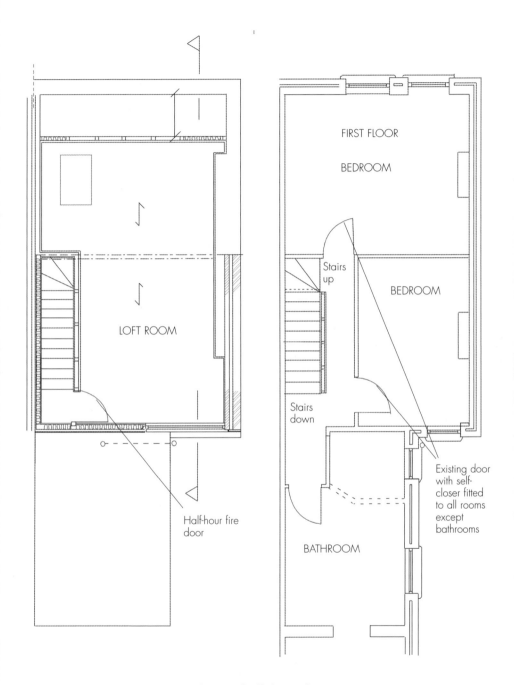

FIRST FLOOR

BEDROOM

Stairs
up

BEDROOM

LOFT ROOM

Stairs
down

Existing door
with self-
closer fitted
to all rooms
except
bathrooms

Half-hour fire
door

BATHROOM

Fire doors and self-closing doors.

to your house, especially when the loft room is a bedroom. Your new staircase should come up from the landing or lobby area below, and not from within another room – for one thing it is an undesirable selling point to have a loft room that can only be accessed via another bedroom, and from a safety aspect it could leave you trapped up there should a fire break out downstairs. It is much better to have your stairs enclosed throughout the house so that you can pass straight down to the hall and front door, even if this means hiving off part of an existing room with partitioning to accommodate the new stairs. The Building Regulations 2000 include this within the approved document on fire safety.

Space-saving stairs, with a steep, almost ladder-like pitch and paddle-shaped treads, can be used if space is too limited for a normal staircase. With alternating treads, however, this does mean that you have to start off on the right foot if you are going to make it to the other end safely.

8. Do I have to have fire doors fitted throughout my home?

For two-storey homes, fitting discreet self-closing devices to the existing doors on the landings and hall that help to contain a fire by keeping doors shut, together with a new fire-rated door to the loft storey, are common requirements of Building Regulations.

Effectively, a half-hour-rated fire door must separate the new floor from the remainder of your home, although the door can be located at the bottom of the new stairs if there isn't room at the top.

Fire doors are available in a variety of finishes with domestic appearances, so don't worry that it will look like an office door. The same goes for the self-closer – those overhead bulky ones needn't be used when discrete chain closers can be fitted into the back edge of the door, and even rising butts can be used as hinges.

The door should be fitted with smoke seals to prevent smoke penetrating the new floor.

9. Can I bring some daylight into the stair enclosure with glazed partitions or doors?

Forming an enclosed, fire-protected stairway through your home needn't mean creating a dark shaft bereft of natural light. Glass partitions or glass in doors could be used in a two- or three-storey conversion if it were fire-resistant to at least 30 minutes standard. It needn't be the mega-expensive insulating fireproof glass that is used in shopping centres – in this situation normal Georgian-wired or clear fire-rated glass of the non-insulating type is acceptable. But architecturally wire-reinforced glass can look a bit – well, like a public lavatory. The best way to light your extended stairwell is with windows to the outside, or if you're stuck with it being on an inner wall, then with a skylight window to the top.

10. Where will the water tanks and pipes go?

Water tanks carry a considerable weight, and unless you intend to replumb the entire house and install a combination boiler, you will need to find a new home for them. The space behind the ashlaring where the tanks can be supported by the new floor joists will be ideal. It's a good idea to provide yourself with a few access doors to this residual space anyway so that you can utilise it for storage.

If your loft is to contain a bathroom, however, the cold water tank must be positioned high enough to provide adequate water pressure, and this may mean locating it beneath the apex of the roof. Long, thin tanks, commonly known as 'coffin tanks', are often utilised for such situations. Either way, check that your designer has allowed for their weight in the structural design, as it may not be easy to find a home for them as an afterthought.

Fire safety

The Building Regulations have always contained relaxations or special rules for loft conversions when it comes to fire safety, and of course those rules are prone to some changes as time goes by. Make sure you or your designer are aware of the current requirements; at present the reduced standards only apply to lofts with up to two new rooms (not including bathrooms or dressing rooms), and where the new storey is less than 50 sq m in floor area.

Starting – first things first

Nearly always, the first tradesman to commence work in an attic conversion is the plumber.

Once the old insulation material has been bagged up and removed from the attic, the plumber can make any

necessary alterations, albeit temporary ones, to the water services. Often this will mean relocating the water tanks if they are currently in the middle of the loft space, and deconstructing their support stands.

Until the plumbing services are sorted out, the new floor cannot be fully constructed, hence some co-operation is needed between the plumber and carpenter as to where tanks are to be temporarily positioned and so forth.

Where long steel beams are proposed in the conversion, it may be easiest to allow the builders to make a modest hole in an external gable end wall to feed the beams in. This is often preferable to jointing the beam from shorter lengths within the loft, or manhandling it through the house.

Some enlargement of the trap hatch will probably be considered, but generally it is advisable to cut out the plasterboard ceiling only where the new staircase is to be positioned. It is unlikely to be possible to trim the joists themselves at such an early stage, but once the floor joists are in this can be done, making access easier.

If you have a large dormer or rooflight opening proposed, once this is formed you could insist that all materials and labour come in through the opening from an external scaffold before the windows are fitted. This will reduce the mess inside your home.

The sequence of work

A loft conversion is a major structural alteration to your home and one that can only be done safely and efficiently

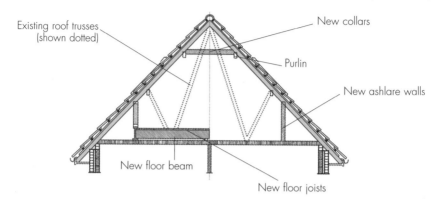

Transforming the roof structure.

if the work is carried out in the right order. It is not the place to be wearing seven-league boots.

Although the structure of roofs can vary tremendously, the sequence in which they are converted doesn't. The basic principles are the same, and the following sequence should apply in general to any loft conversion.

Step 1
CHECK THE EXISTING STRUCTURE
The first step should be to expose the existing foundations, beams and lintels that are proposed to carry the weight of the converted roof. Their adequacy will need to be established, and if they are judged to be insufficient they will need to be strengthened or even replaced.

In some cases it might be possible to redesign the new structure to divert load away from vulnerable areas of the building. The Building Control Officer and your designing engineer may wish to inspect these elements early on, and should be notified once the beams or whatever have been exposed.

Step 2
SUPPORT
Structural work to lofts should always start at the bottom and work up, building in the support as it goes and as the design specifies. That could mean installing any ground floor support beams, posts or walls before starting work in the loft itself.

Step 3
PREPARING THE LOFT
This involves exposing the joists by lifting any existing loft boarding and insulation and removing them from the loft space. Lofts make for very small building sites and have to be kept tidy if work is to proceed safely and efficiently, so be wary of builders who leave the loft littered with waste and materials – the latter should only be brought up when needed, and should not be stored up there.

Step 4
ALTERING THE PLUMBING

Some degree of plumbing alteration is likely if you have water tanks in your loft, and although the new tank supports and positions may not be available yet, the existing ones may be in the way and need to be temporarily repositioned. It should always be possible to keep hot water and heating services working during the conversion, although some temporary disruption (about one day) should be expected.

Step 5
INSTALLING THE NEW FLOOR STRUCTURE

Bringing any new floor beams into position obviously requires access somewhere, and this may not necessarily be through the loft hatch. Sometimes, builders may choose to bring in heavy steel beams through a hole made in the end gable wall or the roof itself. Either way the floor structure must be the first element constructed, and all floor joists together with their supporting beams should be installed before any of the structural roof timbers are cut or removed.

Once the new floor joists are installed, a floor decking will need to be put down to allow the tradesmen to work safely – you can only do so much balancing between joists before somebody gets hurt or a foot comes through the ceiling. Don't be troubled by laying the finished floor boarding yet; it will have to come up to allow the new water pipes and electric cables

through underneath. Indeed, as there is a risk of the boards getting wet when the roof is opened up for the dormer or rooflight windows, it is normal to use plywood sheets at this stage to form a temporary floor cover.

Because the opening for the new stair will be formed now, improved access for workmen and materials can be made at this stage.

This sequence is pretty well universal, but you can decide on whether you want access to the conversion work to be via the house or via the roof window – this goes for both workmen and materials. Either option has some bearing on the sequence, since the opening should coincide with the work but remain weatherproof and secure.

Step 6
INSTALLING THE SUPPORT TO THE RAFTERS

Installing the walls and beams that offer support to the rafters is next on the list. This is likely to include ashlaring (load-bearing) stud walls and any rafter level beams that are designed to transfer the weight of the roof covering to the walls or floor joists. It may also include a ridge beam or new rafters to run alongside the old ones if they need some help. Remember that the rafters are in part going to carry a plasterboard ceiling and insulation, so there will be extra load on them.

Step 7
WINDOW CONSTRUCTION

If your conversion includes dormer windows, the roof

Rooflight installation.

tiles in this area will be removed and the rafters cut to open up the roof for the construction of the dormers.

The support to the dormers either from the floor joists or rafters should already be in place to enable them to be built up swiftly and the dormer roof formed. Obviously this is the vulnerable bit where you become exposed to the elements, and for a short while a tarpaulin becomes part of your roof. In an ideal world you would only carry out this stage when the weather forecast gave you at least three clear days without rain.

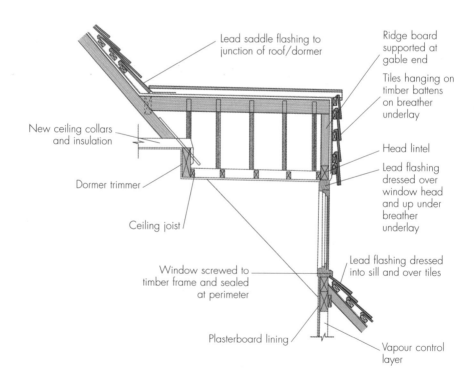

Section showing dormer window construction.

Rooflights are much quicker to install than dormers and come in kit form with everything you need to do the job in one day, so the risk of suffering from the adversities of the weather isn't nearly so great.

Step 8
WEATHERING

Now that the structural work is complete, the roof and dormers can be weathered with their permanent coverings. If there is some delay with hanging tiles or cladding boards, or if the weather is too cold for rendering, then the dormer cheeks may be left boarded with plywood and felted for the time being. This should be enough to keep the weather out and allow the work to progress inside.

Dormer windows themselves can be fitted and glazed, or if building materials are being brought in this way, then they can be left with sheeting covering the opening for the time being. Obviously security is important, and even the stairwell opening to the floor needs to be covered by fixed boarding at the end of each day if you're not to be left vulnerable.

Step 9
INTERNAL FINISHES

With the home now sealed against the elements, internal stud partitions that are not load-bearing can be built, the walls and ceilings can be insulated and lined with plasterboard, after the first-fix electrical and plumbing work is completed. The final floor covering can be fixed down and the staircase installed.

Step 10
FIXTURES AND FITTINGS

Bathroom fittings and the final plumbing connections can be made now, and the bathroom walls tiled as required. Radiators, light fittings and extractor fans, particularly of the recessed type, should be left unfixed to allow decorating to continue behind them as much as possible. Any special floor coverings of tiling, carpets or boarding should be left until last if possible, to avoid being damaged by decorating. Floor boarding, however, is best covered and pinned down by the skirting boards rather than being held by beading run around the edges of the floor, and so skirtings need to be left off until the boards are down.

Protecting the work

Do not allow your builders to drag materials in through fitted skylight windows – or any windows, come to that – unless some protective covering is given to the frame to prevent it from damage. Staircases can be afforded the same care and consideration by taping cardboard to the treads while workmen are still tramping to and fro.

Items like this could be included as conditions of contract, under the heading of 'protection to the works', but if it's too late to do this, then it is only the work of a few minutes plus some old cardboard boxes and masking tape to do it yourself.

Underpinning the foundations

Bungalows tend to have a disadvantage on the structural side: with no floor to support, they were commonly built without any internal load-bearing walls. This presents something of a black hole to designers preparing the plans and calculations, who often need to rely on some internal support to make their structural designs work. The issue as to whether the walls are or aren't load-bearing usually becomes critical once work begins, simply because the designer has left it to the builder to expose the foundations and see if there are any. The floor joists, for example, may have to be supported on them if it is too far for them to span from outside wall to outside wall. The only way to be certain that the wall is capable of carrying the weight is to inspect it, and in particular check what it is sitting on. This means digging a small hole in the floor alongside the wall and checking to see if it has a sound foundation.

If the floor is a suspended timber one, then the operation of lifting a few floorboards and looking to see if the wall continues beneath them will be the place to start. It may be necessary then to see, by digging alongside, if it has a concrete foundation of acceptable thickness and width to spread the weight to the ground.

The same applies to a solid ground floor slab, but in this case if the wall is supported directly on to the slab and does not extend through it, it is normally considered to be non-load-bearing. Unless the concrete slab is of unusual thickness and the loads are light, this is likely to be unacceptable and the wall may have to be underpinned with a proper foundation. This sounds drastic, but it isn't that

uncommon – internal walls are often built as non-load-bearing partitions of brick or blockwork and need underpinning before the true structural work on the loft can begin. Your only way of avoiding this is to request your designers to rely solely on the external walls for support if they can. On the positive side, the subsoil under the buildings is usually dry and compacted, and hence the foundation depth and size can be much less than they are on the outer walls.

Underpinning can be necessary, even for the external walls, if the existing foundations are not up to the job. This is quite a labour-intensive operation to say the least, and although many people are prepared to underpin a single wall to support a converted loft, having to underpin all the walls is not so popular and, in my experience, rarely necessary.

Underpinning is carried out in bays, one piece at a time. A new foundation pit is dug alongside and then beneath the existing, that also undermines it for its full width. The length of this pit or bay depends on the sequence and number of bays you adopt, but typically, it would be between 1 and 2 m long. Obviously the work has to be done piecemeal like this to maintain the stability of the house, particularly as the wall itself cannot be temporarily supported and must span over each hole as it is dug.

The bays are either shuttered at the sides to form a key, or steel reinforcing bars are pushed into the earth at the sides and left protruding to become encased in concrete. When the bay alongside it is dug later, the key or bars are exposed to bond in the next section of foundation concrete, joining it all together. Because concrete shrinks when it hardens, a gap will be left between the new foundation and the old, which is dry-packed later with a dry and fine mix of concrete. Only then will the new foundation accept the weight imposed on it.

Of course this dry-packing can't be done until the concrete is properly hardened, and so the process of underpinning is quite slow. Not only that, but much, if not all, of the digging must be done by hand. For external foundations, the depth of underpinning will depend on factors such as the subsoil condition, whether there are trees nearby affecting the soil, and the risk of ground frost.

Internal underpinning is likely to be much shallower since there is no frost penetration and the subsoil is likely to be desiccated and compact from years of being trapped beneath the building inside the outer wall foundations. Often it is case of digging in only enough to cast a decent thickness of concrete (for a strip foundation, 225–300 mm thick is normal).

In some cases structural posts that support the ends of beams may be included in the design, and these posts may be looking for support in the way of an existing or new foundation. A square or pad foundation is normally what is adopted for these, but the work of digging through the floor to find the natural ground remains the same.

As a home-owner living in your house while conversion works are underway, underpinning is about as disruptive as building work gets. and you would be well advised to discover at an early stage whether or not it is necessary.

The local Building Control Authority may have original plans of your home showing how it was designed, and you might be able to view them at their offices. Neighbours with homes built at the same time to the same design may know about the load-bearing nature of the walls. Look for people in your street who have already converted their lofts, because this issue will almost certainly have come up at the time.

Structure

You have to start from the basic understanding that they didn't make it easy for you. In Britain we have never built our homes with the idea that one day somebody might want to convert the roof space to live in. In other countries, like France, they have.

Over there, chalet bungalows are often built from new with the structure in place to convert the roof. All the owner has to do is add a stair, finishings and electrics. The building is already constructed to take it, with even the windows pre-installed, lighting the attic and waiting. They seem to recognise that the young couple who bought the place as a starter-home bungalow might one day start a family and need to expand their home. We can only imagine such forward thinking from our developers. Even as recently as 1997, statistics showed that only 4 per cent of our new homes were designed to make use of the roof space,

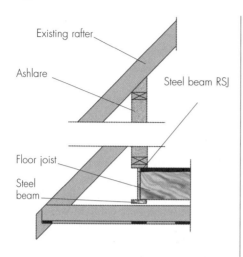

Steel beam support to ashlare and floor

and most of them were constructed with it already converted to maximise the developers' profits.

There is a school of thought, a sceptical one perhaps, that suggests that house developers in the UK have been getting away with murder for decades, providing us with low-quality boxes that inhibit our chances of extending them and urge us to dispose and trade up to the next, slightly larger low-quality box on the property ladder – a bit like the new car that you can't fix yourself but can't live with forever, either.

To make matters worse, developers in the 1960s sought to reduce building costs and started using prefabricated roof trusses with a web of diagonals and a lower pitch. They weren't exactly thinking about loft conversions when they started this trend, and 40 years on they still aren't. For all these reasons, it should be clear that nobody has made

it easy for you to convert your loft. That doesn't mean to say you can't. Britain has seen well over a million loft conversions, and millions more lofts are capable of being converted.

On the plus side, trussed roofs on new homes tend to be of a much steeper pitch these days for improved weather resistance and better aesthetics, so the headroom is often there for a room in the roof.

One other drawback of any trussed rafter roof conversion is the fact the existing roof normally spans from wall plate to wall plate without any support in the middle. Without load-bearing support walls in the middle, the conversion will be made more complex and hence more expensive.

In a two-storey house, the upper floor will usually have been supported on some load-bearing ground floor partitions, but these may not have been extended to the first floor in the same construction – if at all. The work of bringing up the load-bearing structure from the ground through existing walls, studwork partitions, or by strengthening non-load-bearing partitions is often needed to overcome this problem. It may be that all that is required is a load-bearing post here and there, built into a studwork partition to carry the ends of beams. These posts, if they are extra timber posts in a studwork partition, are sometimes referred to as 'cripple studs' because they act like splints.

Faced with no partitions on the first floor that you can employ, maybe because they are in the wrong place, or because they are just supported from

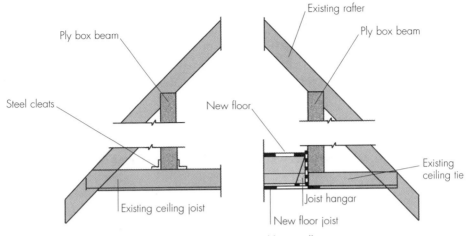

Box beams as ashlare walls.

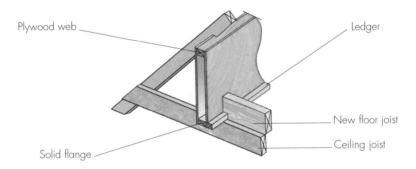

Plywood box beam.

the floor joists themselves, and you have only one option – beams. Big beams or beams of varying type, but beams all the same.

Faced with using very deep beams, supported from the external walls only, it is usually thought of as a pretty neat idea to locate them within the ashlare walls themselves, where they can be hidden and their size isn't on show. The ashlare walls can then be built off the top of them, and the floor

joists can be spun into the web or hung off the side. This cunning plan works fine where you have ashlare walls available on both sides of the roof, but if you want a dormer window on one or both sides, it runs short of being a perfect idea. The beam may have to protrude above the floor line here, with the floor stepped up to a raised section or dais to 'design it in'.

Be wary of keeping the window openings up and the cill not less than

73

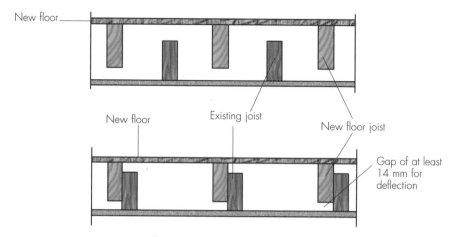

New floor joists alongside existing ones.

800 mm off the floor if you are faced with accepting this option. You don't want the raised floor to be a used as a diving platform out of the window.

As an alternative to ashlare walls, plywood box beams or even metal lattice beams can be installed. Box beams can be made up on-site with plywood glued around a softwood frame to an engineer's design. Where they are used, they can support the rafters as well the new floor joists and enable work to proceed swiftly. Alternatively, metal lattice beams can be made up from angle iron that looks rather like a gantry for a crane. They have the disadvantage of having to be manufactured off-site, usually at a steel fixers, but have the advantage of being lighter than steel beams over the same span. They thus tend to be used where a long span would mean a steel beam

	MAXIMUM SPAN OF FLOOR JOISTS	
JOIST SIZE	400 MM CRS	600 MM CRS
50 x 125 mm	2.65 m	2.29 m
50 x 150 mm	3.19 m	2.78 m
50 x 175 mm	3.67 m	3.21 m
50 x 200 mm	4.20 m	3.68 m
50 x 225 mm	4.71 m	4.14 m

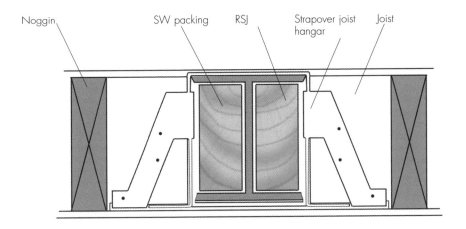

Floor beam RSJ with joists supported on strap-over-type hangars.

in that position would be too heavy.

Personally, I don't like the use of steel beams of any description in loft conversions if they can be avoided. Timber is a far better material for roofs – it is lighter, natural and can be easily fixed into position and fixed into.

Obviously it has its limitations in how much weight it can carry, and it is only commonly available in certain sizes. The table on page 74 gives some indication of what size timber is needed for what length of floor joist. Two joist centres are shown, 400 mm and

---

LOFT WALL HEIGHTS

The table below uses basic trigonometry to show what sort of ashlare wall height you will have given different roof pitches when it is positioned 1 m in from the wall plate. For structural joists to be designed to carry ashlare walls and roof loads via them, the ashlare needs to be located around this distance and not too far in from the joist bearings.

Roof pitch	Ashlare height
30°	0.55 m
35°	0.70 m
40°	0.84 m
45°	1.00 m
50°	1.19 m

600 mm. Timber grade C24 (aka SC4 or SS) is used, as it has the advantage of being stronger and less shrinkable than C16. For these reasons it should be employed in loft conversion work. The table assumes C24 timber and joists carrying standard domestic floor loads only, and does not allow for the weight of any partitions, load-bearing or otherwise. It does take into account the fact that sawn timber joist sizes will be less than the dimensions shown.

There is a compromising solution between timber and steel beams which designers can adopt and do so in this kind of work – flitch beams.

Flitch beams

These beams are a hybrid of the two materials, combined like a sandwich to produce a beam that can be made up on-site, is easily fixed to, and is stronger than wood alone. Flitch beams consist of two timbers bolted together with a mild steel plate sandwiched in the middle (see diagram below). The steel plate can range from 6 mm to 25 mm thick and be of a similar depth to the timbers, but typically it is 25 mm shorter to accommodate shrinkage in the wood. With flitch beams the bolting is critical, and the bolts are normally staggered along the length of the beam at between 300 mm and 400 mm centres. The design of flitch beams has not always been accepted, particularly by London District Surveyors (Building Control Officers' former capital title), but they have proved to be a popular and effective solution since the 1980s to many design problems and are now commonly used.

Building up the floor joists

Lofts that have been badly or illegally converted often have one common feature – the ceiling joists have been enlarged to become floor joists. This

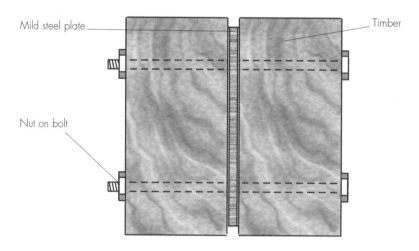

Mild steel plate

Timber

Nut on bolt

Flitch beam.

has often been done by nailing on extra 50 x 100 mm joists to the top of the existing ceiling joists, attempting to make them into 50 x 200 mm floor joists. Not a good idea. In theory it might be possible to do this, but only if the two timbers are perfectly smooth and level-faced, so that they can be seamlessly glued and screwed together to act as one. In the real world we call this unlikely, if not impossible.

Although this frequently happens with DIY or cowboy conversions, it is worth mentioning, because even qualified architects and structural engineers sometimes design things that work on paper and are based on sound theory, but stop short of being practicable or even possible. Yes, it is nice to see the boundaries of science being pushed by innovative design, but do you really want your home to be a testing ground for new ideas?

I prefer to leave the architecture separate from the structure when it comes to a home loft conversion. I believe the structure should be as simple as it can be, whilst still conforming with the known, tried and tested methods of construction. Leave the experiments to bridges across the Thames and simulated gardens of Eden.

Raised collars or ties

Cut and pitched roofs often incorporate tie beams, known as collars, that cross your roof space fixing together rafters on opposite sides. By doing this they are helping to prevent the roof from spreading. Collars tend to be placed around mid-span in older properties, and there is no way of working around

Ridge beam positioned beneath barge board.

them – they have to come out. To compensate for them, raised collars are often installed below the ridge but high enough to form a flat ceiling overhead.

If you are adopting an ashlare wall construction to support the rafters, they too can be used to help reduce the spread of the roof along with the new higher and shorter collars. It helps if the connections between these elements are bolted or employ metal fixings, which will be more effective than simple nailed joints.

If you don't have the headroom even for raised collars, a ridge beam is often installed directly under the apex of the roof and running through its entire length. A beam in this position acts a bit like a tent pole with the roof hanging from it, and in doing so it reduces the outward thrust (the spread) of the roof.

Once the structural work is complete and before any boards or finishings are fixed down covering it up, check that the layout, member sizes and fixings used are in accordance with the design. Your Building Control Surveyor should also be invited in now to do the same.

Fire safety

So, moving upwards into the loft is the easy answer to finding new living space in our homes, but in moving upwards you reduce your chances of escaping or being rescued in a fire, unless you have designed in some effective precautions against fire.

It is difficult to think of our homes as anything other than a safe place of refuge and comfort, so it isn't easy to imagine the risk of a fire breaking out, and it's even harder to consider how you could become fatally trapped in your own sanctuary, but the sad truth is that every year people are. In 1999 alone over 72,000 homes caught fire in the UK, killing 466 people and injuring a further 14,600. In fact these statistics show that most (between 70 and 80 per cent) deaths from fire do occur at home, often when people are asleep and unaware of the danger.

Two-storey to three-storey

It is also the case that if we move our living space and particularly our bedrooms higher, we move ourselves further away from the safety of the ground floor exits and escape in the event of a fire. Converting the loft in a two-storey house means adding a third floor, an extra level above the ground and the risks that that includes invokes extra fire safety requirements that don't exist in bungalows or two-storey homes. It has always been considered that you may be fairly easily rescued by ladder from the window of a first floor, but the window of a second floor and particularly a roof window is another matter. As a result, Building Regulations

Centre-hung rooflight – not suitable for escape

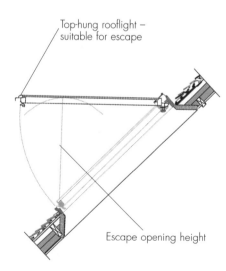

Top-hung rooflight – suitable for escape

Escape opening height

Centre-pivot rooflight (left) and top-hung rooflight (right).

have always sought to require a safe and protected way out down through the building when we find ourselves at high level. The problem is, many of our homes weren't designed with the stairs leading down to the front door inside a hallway or reception room, and worse still some, (like mine) were built with the stairs leading down into the lounge.

If you are fortunate enough to have a home on a sloping site where the outside ground is much higher on one side than another, it would be extremely wise to locate escape windows on the side above the high ground. If you have solid roofs from single storey extensions below windows, these too can be used to make escape easier.

To take account of the varying nature of houses and outside ground, heights have been quoted in the legislation controlling this work. The figure of 4.5 m for a floor above ground level is the point at which additional fire safety measure are introduced. Effectively this means most two-storey homes will have their new loft room at this level or above and will require upgrading.

Single-storey to two-storey (bungalow conversion)

So what is an economical loft to convert? Bungalows with cut and pitched roofs built in the first half of the twentieth century are ideal. For one thing, with a bungalow you are transforming your home into a two-storey property (a chalet bungalow to an estate agent, but a two-storey property to the rest of us), and it will not invoke the fire requirements that

are unpopular with many people.

You won't be needing fire doors, a fire-protected stairway or even self-closing devices on the existing doors – things that can turn delivering breakfast in bed into an assault course. You will still need smoke alarms and window openings that are useable for potential escape, but that's about all in fire-safety requirements.

The chances are you won't need to upgrade the ceiling fire-protection either to the new floor above, since you don't need a full half-hour fire-resistance as you do with three-storey loft conversions. Not only are bungalow lofts cheaper to convert with this reduced specification, but they are usually more profitable to do and can increase the house's value dramatically.

Three storeys to four storeys (town house or mews conversion)

At the other end of the scale, three-storey townhouses or mews houses with shallow trussed roofs are probably the least suitable. Where the height of the new loft floor occurs at 7.5 m or more above the ground, then at least two staircases, separate from each other, are needed. Converting the loft in a three-storey town house or mews can sometimes invoke this requirement because you are effectively creating a fourth storey (a mini-block of flats), so you may well need a second staircase serving the top floor. Window escape or rescue is no longer an option above 4.5 m, and two stairs are expected by the Building Regulations.

On the positive side, if your three-storey home is of recent construction, it will have been built already with a protected stairway plus fire doors and won't need upgrading any further. It might even be possible to connect one of the new loft room stairs back into the existing stair enclosure at a lower level in the building, instead of taking it through to ground level.

I tend to think that an external stair might be the last resort, but one serving a balcony formed within the roof by what is known as an inverted dormer could work nicely.

Picture a mews house loft room with full-height french doors opening out onto a small balcony deck wind-sheltered on both sides by the sloping faces of the roof, guarded by balustrading that also encloses a spiral stair twisting down to a roof deck or balcony below that leads back into the house. The idea behind this is that if you want to live at this height, you might as well appreciate the view.

Existing ceilings

As for the new floor in two- or three-storey conversions, this should have at least 30 minutes' fire-resistance attributed to it, which can mean that the existing ceiling needs upgrading with extra plaster. Even in bungalows, 20 minutes' protection is needed, as this ceiling now protects a floor and not the roof above. If it is plasterboard, then the thickness of the board and any finish to it should be checked to see if it is sufficient. An easy remedy if it isn't is to apply a PVA adhesive to create a bond and have a skim finish plastered on to the ceiling to upgrade it.

If it isn't plasterboard, it is most probably plaster and lath. Homes built before the 1940s have these ceilings, which comprise of plaster adhering to thin timber laths, and at the least it needs to be still adhering. If it isn't, or if the ceiling is damaged, the chances are it is going to need replacing with plasterboard. Many lath-and-plaster ceilings become damaged during building work, as any vibrations or accidental wetting can damage the bond between the two, thus causing them to separate.

Sprinklers

You are not going to need to install a domestic sprinkler system into your home, unless you want to. I can see you thinking that you would have to be criminally insane to want to – the damage was bad enough when you accidentally burst a central heating pipe pinning the carpet down, wasn't it? – but in other countries, such as Australia and the USA, they do install them. Indeed, in some places there it has been required by local building law in the construction of new houses for many years, making huge reductions in their fire losses.

I mention this only because if you are confronted by structural fire precaution requirements that you simply can't live with or accommodate, then a sprinkler system, installed in accordance with the code of practice, may be an acceptable alternative for you and the Building Control Authority. It could mean that your staircase can remain open plan from the lounge area and that you don't require self-closers on all the doors.

I confess that I have yet to meet anyone who has gone for this option, but you should know that it exists – and it might not be as bad as you think. The pipework for a system would have to run through the floor voids like your central heating pipes already do. If your mains water pressure is good, you won't need a separate storage tank (which you probably haven't got the space for anyway, if you're converting the loft). You might only need one or two sprinkler heads on the ceiling of each room, and the ones that have a plate covering them fit quite flush to the ceiling and can be painted to make them almost invisible. The manufacturers will tell you that they hardly ever go off accidentally (they would, wouldn't they?), but perhaps more importantly, when a fire does occur they discharge a fraction of the amount that the fire brigade will use when they arrive.

Sprinklers have a good track record of putting out fires, since the heads can have heat detectors that activate them individually and hence precisely over the fire at an early stage in its development. The reason that they aren't mandatory in Britain is because that our controls have always related to saving people rather than buildings, the latter being traditionally what sprinklers have been used for. They cost, allegedly, about the same as installing a central heating system.

Smoke alarms

Whatever the benefits or otherwise of sprinklers, they shouldn't be used in lieu of smoke alarms.

Smoke can kill us before a fire has reached a high temperature, and before we have even woken up. So alarms that give us an early warning have proven to be an essential ingredient in our homes, giving us vital minutes to escape before things get serious.

When it comes to providing smoke alarms during building work, mains-powered models should be used with a battery back-up that will cut in and sustain the unit if the electrical supply is taken out. These used to be quite expensive, but now they have come down to the extent that they are only moderately more pricey than the battery ones on sale in DIY stores. You will soon recoup the extra cost on fewer batteries, and the permanent protection to you and your family will be priceless.

Mains units should be interlinked so that they talk to each other and when one goes off, they all go off. It is generally considered normal to wire them in from the domestic lighting circuit, and providing you have that rechargeable battery back-up type, this is fine. Otherwise, they can be connected back to the fuseboard on a separate protected circuit.

A mains-wired smoke alarm fixed to the ceiling of your loft storey is best placed on the ceiling on the landing and should be interlinked to other units on the landing and hall below. The position of the detector should be such that it will wake you when activated by smoke entering the stair enclosure, and for this reason you ought to test its audibility with the fire door shut. Make sure your electrician doesn't stick alarms in smoke black spots like close to walls or pendant light fittings. Smoke alarms save lives, and if more of them were mains-powered, without the risk of the old batteries being left unreplaced, they would save more.

Stairs in bungalows

So we've established that you don't need that protected stairway in a bungalow loft conversion, but you still have to find room for the stairs in a building that was never meant to have them. The hallway behind the front door is the ideal place, but is it wide enough to accommodate a stair and still let you in?

Where it hasn't been wide enough some people have chosen to block up the front door altogether, put a window in the opening instead and rely solely on the back door to get in and out of the house. In doing so you would be effectively making all the rooms into inner rooms that you can only escape from by passing through the house from the back door (and often the kitchen – a likely place for a fire to start). Besides, making the back door and kitchen the receptionist of your home through which all social and business callers must pass isn't ideal. On the bright side you are going to deter double-glazing salesmen, but aside from that I can't suggest that this is ever a good idea. In fact, I'm certain it must be suicide from a Feng Shui point of view.

No, there is a price to pay for converting bungalows, and it is this: you must lose some space on the ground floor to house the stairs, and often that means hiving off part of a room by the entrance hall. Not an easy thing to do when you are trying to gain space, not lose it, but the stairs really need to lead up away from the front door and arrive at a point of maximum headroom beneath the apex of the roof. If the headroom just isn't available here because of the slope of the roof, then a dormer window built out over the stairs will increase it. Just leave the front door alone or build in a new one.

Stair design

An 'off the shelf' standard flight of a stairs is the cheapest option and probably the safest when it comes to it, but you might not have the room to fit it in. Try hard to, however, before you scrap the idea and go for a purpose-made stair – the price difference will be considerable, and you may end up with a stair so full of turns and winders that you find it uncomfortable to use and impossible to get the furniture up.

Having said that, with a little care the staircase can be a focal point, a feature of architectural delight. Take balusters, for example – leave it to the builder to decide what you want, and you will get square balusters and square newel posts, finishing with a mop handle-shaped handrail. Functional – yes, masculine – certainly, architectural – no, attractive – never. Balusters come in different styles, different wood, chamfered, twisted … any of which may render a plain staircase beautiful, and all of which will be an improvement.

Search the catalogues of specialist joinery companies and choose for

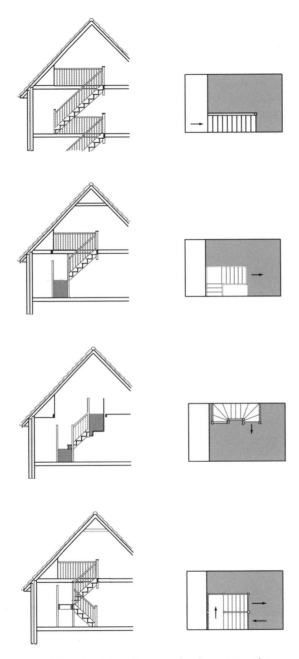

From top to bottom: straight stair; stair with quarter-landing; stair with two quarter-turn winders; stair with half-landing.

yourself; never leave it to the builder to decide on the stairs.

Alternate-tread stairs

Alternate-tread stairs are the space-saving type with paddle-shaped treads that allow the stair construction to overlap and rise more steeply than a normal stair. They are often marketed for loft conversion use since space for a second stair is often tight. I think on average these stairs only need about 1.5 m on plan (that is to say measured horizontally) to get from top to bottom, compared to a normal stair's 2.7 m. As open-riser stairs with paddle treads, they can't be carpeted and are usually made from pine.

Usually purchased as flat packs complete with fixings for you to put together like Swedish furniture, they are widely used, although personally, they frighten the life out of me. I do not have the benefit of a choreographic history that allows me to dance down any staircase, and really I need to come down them facing the stair itself like a ladder. You're probably more co-ordinated than me, limb-wise, and will be able to start off on the correct foot, placing each accurately on half (the other half is missing) of a smooth-

Alternate-tread staircase.

Extending ladder.

sanded pine tread as you go, making it to the bottom in one piece.

I find ordinary stairs hazardous enough without introducing a game show element to them, but they do comply with the Building Regulations and can be used as access stairs for lofts where space is too tight for a normal stair. Because of their unique shape, these stairs should only be used where a single habitable room is provided in the loft, although an accompanying bathroom would be an acceptable alternative.

Retractable ladders

The next step (excuse the pun) down from an alternate tread stair is the extending ladder – the sort of folding or sliding ladder that drops down fixed to the back of the loft hatch. These are not suitable or permitted by regulations where the loft is being converted. They can be used where you are simply improving the roof space for storage and not a habitable room, and so if you are planning to do this, they make an ideal choice.

The door, ladder and frame come as part of the package designed to fit between roof trusses 600 mm apart. Structural trimming can only be done on a cut and pitched roof where ceiling joists may be 400 mm apart, and in these cases the ceiling joists can be cut and properly trimmed. Trussed rafters cannot be cut, even at ceiling level, to make way for loft hatches.

Loft hatch doors come as insulated now, a modern-day requirement. The amount of room you have around the loft hatch is critical with the

retractable ladders which lie flat in the roof, but the folding type require less storage space. Since they both are designed to drop down with the hinged hatch door, they need opening with some care and respect if the excitement of having them descend suddenly towards you is to be avoided.

Daylight and windows

Loft rooms have the potential for being the brightest rooms in the home. By installing rooflights in the sloping parts of the ceiling, a room can be flooded with daylight throughout the day. Even on overcast days the light gain from a rooflight window is considerable – and far superior to that of a window that is located in a wall.

Rooflights can let in up to 40 per cent more daylight than a conventional dormer window, and daylight is important to us. We should aim to provide a bare minimum of 10 per cent of the floor area in window area to light it, but most of us would like to see twice that, if not more.

Traditional dormer windows may have more character than rooflights, and they have the advantage of maximising headroom, but they don't let in so much light. In conservation situations this may be more of a problem, since the dormer windows are often smaller in older buildings and your planning authority may require you to maintain the character of the house or area by keeping them in scale. A hipped dormer roof and tile hanging to the cheeks looks effective from the outside, but does nothing to help light the room inside.

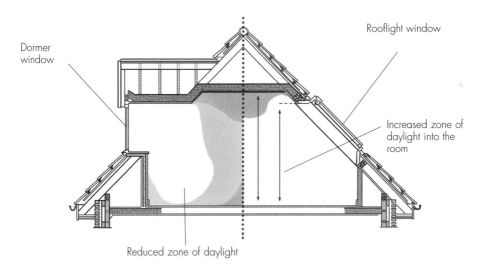

Dormer window

Rooflight window

Increased zone of daylight into the room

Reduced zone of daylight

Differences in light penetration between dormer (left) and roof windows.

On a more modern building, the opportunity may exist for you to fully glaze the dormer cheeks as triangles of glass and adopt a gable end face with glass above the window as well, infilling the gable triangle as it were. Dormers like these are much more effective at lighting a room and have the added benefit of expanding the view to the sides and above.

The proportions of the window have to be watched carefully because they can look a bit like fish tanks protruding from the roof. A tall dormer or square one with a steep roof usually works better than a long oblong one with a shallow roof, but on the whole a dormer bay window like this adds a whole new dimension to a loft room. It will catch sunlight at different times of the day, lighting the room at ceiling level

as well as eye level.

There may be no reason why you should restrict yourself to one or the other; it is quite common for loft conversions to be formed with a dormer window across the back and a rooflight or two at the front. If anything, this approach is the archetypal conversion that addresses the planning authority needs for permitted development, provides half the roof with maximum headroom, but still gives the benefit of some sky lighting.

Providing daylight not just to the rooms but to the stairs is a good idea too. Staircases tend to be forgotten when it comes to lighting, but I can't think of a more sensible place in the house to provide enough light to see by. This is even more important when your stair is enclosed in the loft room by a wall and a door, as it may be for fire protection. Natural light then will save you a fortune on electricity over the years, and what better way to bring it in to the stair enclosure than through a rooflight positioned near the top of the staircase where light can flood in and down the stairs?

As we've already discussed, headroom on stairs is a legal requirement, and if you're struggling to achieve it, including the staircase within a dormer window may be necessary anyway. If it is just a matter of gaining a few inches at a critical spot on the stairs, then perhaps a rooflight will do that just as well by trimming the ceiling line and raising it to the glass level. When it comes to staircase headroom, every little bit counts!

If your home is within a conservation area or is listed, you may have to install a rooflight that is in keeping with the character and age of the building. A dormer window may not be permitted for these reasons, and a modern-style rooflight may be inappropriate too. Because of this, some companies have manufactured conservation-style rooflights that have a lower profile and, in some, an actual glazing bar (not the common dummy bar installed in the double-glazing) within the metal frame to resemble a Victorian cast-iron roof window.

It's important to decide before buying one of these whether or not you will be counting on it for emergency escape in a fire. Some of them are top-hung and openable on a threaded bar, and may only open so far. Others are side-hung and open fully, and can be

Rooflight.

used for escape purposes. They need to have a clear opening space of 850 mm high by 500 mm wide if you are to climb out of them comfortably, and be located reasonably close to the eaves of the roof (no more than 1.7 m away), but not too low to the loft floor. Achieving both is often a juggling act, especially as you don't want to have the window so low that it presents a safety threat to children who, when they're not shoving their heads through railings, have a tendency to climb out of windows Peter-Pan style. 800 mm off the floor is low enough for the bottom cill of a window, but too much higher and you won't be able to get out of it

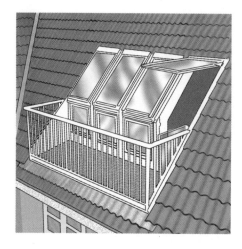 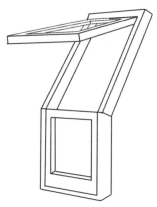

Dual-opening balcony windows for recessed balconies.

easily when you do need to, or reach the eaves once you are out. The pitch or angle of the roof plays a big part here. Too shallow, and it may not be possible to achieve this.

It is always worth considering linking rooflights together to form the appearance of a partially glazed roof rather than dot them about individually. This does, however, present a structural design issue with trimming around the openings, particularly if they are located on the roof.

If you are faced with positioning a rooflight lower than you would like or in a vulnerable position, then you can get opening restrictors fitted. These key-operated devices simply prevent the window from being opened further than about 100 mm so children cannot open them and climb out. Because restrictors need a key to release them, they shouldn't be used where the window acts as an escape window. Hunting for the key won't seem like fun

in an emergency – escape windows need to be immediately openable.

Room with a view

Don't forget that the view out is an important part of locating a window. It is always a bit of a surprise to see the view for the first time from roof level (part of the fun of loft conversions), but try to assess beforehand what it will be like – whether that tree will obscure the line of sight to the sea, or whether that telegraph pole will be smack between your window and the sunset.

If all it means is shifting a window along a foot or two, then it's worth trying to get it right to start with. Your builder will be able to move a window opening, but will almost certainly complain about it and harbour no sympathies for your view whatsoever (I make no apologies for that pun). Ensure that window or rooflight openings are correctly positioned and at the right height, particularly if they are

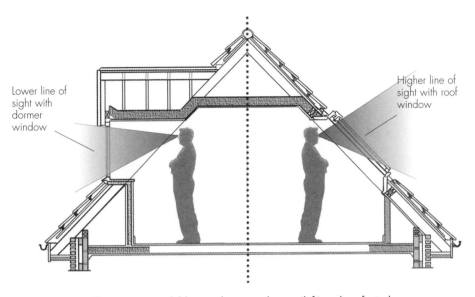

Lower line of sight with dormer window

Higher line of sight with roof window

Differences in available view between dormer (left) and roof windows.

to double as fire exits, before the windows are fitted. It is usually possible to locate rooflights so that you have a view out even from a seated position.

Whether you want the view from a standing or sitting position, whether you want to be able to see straight down, to the side or just plain straight out will have a bearing on the position and type of window you go for. Dormers are good for straight out or straight down, but offer no panorama. Skylights are good for stargazing and straight out, and the wider ones are nice for that widescreen effect, but you can't see down to the street below. Views are important – give some thought to what it is you want to look at from your new lofty position.

Balcony skylight windows that fold out in two pieces with hinged balustrading unfolding to the sides, like something out of *Thunderbirds*, are available for those of us who have a view worth stepping out on the roof to see. They come in different guises, some with a fixed lower pane of glass that just pulls up vertical but doesn't create any extra floor as such, others with side opening lower panels and a balcony, recessed or otherwise.

Extras

Skylight windows can be enhanced with a variety of optional extras these days, from traditional blinds to electric-power opening for those high-level ones. It is even possible to get outside shutter blinds for added security, storm-protection and sound insulation if you live near a flight path or a busy road.

Thermal insulation

The standards for energy conservation

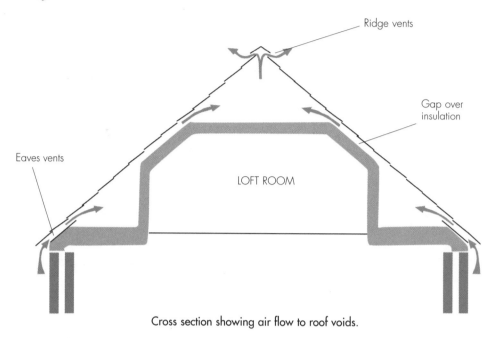

Ridge vents

Gap over insulation

Eaves vents

LOFT ROOM

Cross section showing air flow to roof voids.

have been increased regularly since the 1980s, and the focus has now shifted away from the building of new homes to increasing the energy efficiency of existing ones. The Government have planned to save almost half of all carbon emissions from buildings by 2010 with requirements imposed on our existing homes. They aim to do this with higher insulation standards whenever we extend, convert or alter our homes, and with new legislation to regulate energy use. Even changing your boiler or installing replacement windows now is subject to Building Regulation control.

With loft rooms, insulating them effectively isn't simply about preventing heat loss during the winter, it is also about keeping them cool in summer. Roof voids are always prone

to excessive changes in temperature throughout the year, and if you don't take measures to reduce those changes and maintain a comfortable temperature, you'll be restricting the amount of use and pleasure you get from your new attic room. Insulating loft rooms against heat loss and heat gain can be tricky, but there are a few choices of materials that can make the task somewhat easier.

Whichever way you decide to insulate, the job must be done carefully and with good workmanship during the construction work. Generally, laying the insulation down in the roof space was a job for the labourer on new-build housing, and didn't require any particular skills. Building in insulation for a loft conversion does, and you need to make sure that your builders treat the job with the care and consideration it's due. If they hash the task (as many are prone to do), your finished loft room can suffer from excessive heat loss and damp problems. The damp usually comes from not ventilating the cold air space over the insulation properly, and as a result condensation builds up between the rafter and leaks through.

Roof insulation

Unless you have dormer windows on both sides of your roof that extend to the full length of the room, some part of your loft room will have a sloping ceiling that needs insulating. And because headroom space is at a premium on sloping ceilings, the insulation usually has to be fitted between the rafters as opposed to underneath them. This is where the problems start. You can't simply stuff the gap full of glass-fibre insulation without causing it to sweat and condense water vapour.

To make the structure breathable and allow water vapour to be cleared, you need to allow an air gap of at least 50 mm to exist and cross-ventilate it over the top of the insulation. Cross-ventilating it means letting the air in at one end and out at the other. There are proprietary vents that can be built in to your roof (if they aren't there already) to do this and further advice on those can be found under 'Roof ventilation' in Chapter 6.

Because of the required air gap and the given depth of the rafters that exist, you are already limited in your choice of insulation material. You will have to meet Building Regulations standards (and they get more stringent all the time), and you will want to make your home as energy-efficient as possible.

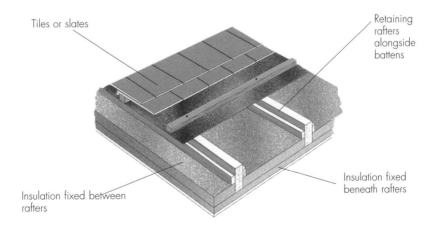

Tiles or slates

Retaining rafters alongside battens

Insulation fixed between rafters

Insulation fixed beneath rafters

Roof insulation between rafters.

I say your home and not just your loft room, because a third of the heat from your whole house goes out through the roof and good insulation up here will make a difference to your home.

Invariably rafters are only 100 mm deep (standard 50 mm x 100 mm), and thus you have only 50 mm left for insulation thickness – not enough for some insulants to meet the regulations. You may need to deepen the space by fixing timber battens to the underside of them, but these really shouldn't be deeper than 50 mm themselves.

If you can't afford to lose the headroom from counter-battening, rigid slab insulants can be fitted in two layers, one between the rafters and one thinner layer beneath them, pinned in position. The plasterboard then has to be fixed through it into the rafters with longer than normal plasterboard screws. There is a limit to this second layer (and it is wise to keep it as thin as possible but still meeting the standards) that has more to do with the length of screws available than anything else.

Because of these logistical problems, insulation to sloping roofs has always received more relaxation to the Building Regulations standards than insulation laid flat within roof voids. Even so, the standards are high and the Government has remained committed to reducing carbon dioxide emissions from our buildings.

Because of these increasing standards, some of the old-type insulation products are not so useable these days. Glass fibre, for example, relied on depth with plenty of air pockets trapped between the fibres to

insulate, the higher the standards go the deeper the insulation needed to meet them. (I didn't like the stuff anyway, those airborne fibres can be breathed in without a mask, and they irritated my skin like hell.)

Polyurethane foam boards aren't much better when you're cutting them – the exposed edges are fibrous and quite sharp, and need treating with a lot of respect. If these boards are being fitted between rafters, a lot of cutting may be needed to ensure a snug fit. With a thermal conductivity value that is much lower than mineral or glass-fibre products, they can be used in much thinner thicknesses to the same result. The measure of any insulation product is its K value (thermal conductivity) which spells out how good it is at stopping heat from passing through it. The lower the K value, the better it is. The numbers are expressions of watts per metre Kelvin, since they are measures of heat over a square metre in a given temperature state and dryness, which means that they are very small numbers basically and not easy to read at a glance.

Rigid polyurethane and phenolic foam (closed-cell) insulation tends to have a K value of between 0.019 and 0.025, much better than that of glass or mineral fibre (open-cell) insulation at between 0.037 and 0.040. Expanded polystyrene (the same product used in packaging) comes in at about 0.037.

These figures are small and the differences between them appear insignificant, but they couldn't have more of an effect on things than they do. To realise this you have to understand that you will get the same amount of insulation from 200 mm of glass fibre as 75 mm of polyurethane foam or 25 mm of multi-layer reflective sheeting. These thicknesses are critical in loft conversions – they make the difference between hitting your head and not hitting your head on the ceiling, and can even decide whether or not you go ahead with the project.

The most high-performing insulation product available at present is multi-layer reflective sheeting material, which may contain as a many as 14 alternating thin layers of reflective aluminium foil, phenolic foam and soft fleecy wadding. Together, though, these amount to a thickness of no more than 25 mm and produce the equivalent amount of insulation in glass fibre quilt eight times as thick. In addition, they appear to have no health threats from airborne fibres or particles, the material can be unrolled, and cut with sharp household scissors and stapled to the underside of the rafters. The joints need to be taped up with special reflective taping, and battens may be called for over the top (lining down the rafters) to create an airspace on the inner surface, so you may still lose 50 mm on the headroom, but those are about the only drawbacks that I can see – that, and the cost of the material, which, being new to the UK and state-of-the-art, is pretty expensive at time of writing.

Wall insulation

Don't forget that if you have a gable-end wall or even a party wall in your loft, they might need insulating themselves. An end-gable cavity wall may well have cavity insulation and the same specification as the walls below, but on the other hand it might not. You'll not be overwhelmed to hear that house builders sometimes save themselves money by doing no more than the bare essentials in construction. If the ceiling level was the insulation level before, then there is every chance that they didn't take the cavity insulation any higher than this in the walls.

You can easily check by drilling a hole internally or looking to see if a cavity tray is built in at ceiling level. The builders would have needed to install a tray DPC above the insulation to make sure that penetrating damp doesn't soak into the top of the insulation, so if such a DPC is visible it is an indication that the insulation starts (or stops) below it. Bear in mind that trays should also exist over lintels for window openings and lean-to roof abutments, regardless of the insulation.

Upgrading an existing end-gable wall is an easy job. From the inside a drywall insulation board can be fitted and plasterboarded over 50 mm thickness of insulation should be enough to upgrade any cavity wall to an acceptable standard, so long as you use either mineral-fibre or urethane/phenolic foam boards with conductivity no worse than 0.037 wattage per metre squared by degrees Kelvin.

You won't need so much insulation on a party wall with a cold roof space on the other side, but some insulation will certainly help. 25 mm of phenolic or urethane foam board and plasterboard finishing will upgrade a party wall of two skins of brickwork up to a 'U' value of 0.55 w/m2K.

You can buy polyurethane or phenolic foam board prelaminated on one side with plasterboard to make the job easier. It is then only a matter of securing it to the wall on adhesive dabs and finishing the joints.

Alternatively, the wall can be framed out with 50 mm timber battens and the insulation pinned between them. The plasterboard can then be nailed to the battens. I say plasterboard, but you might choose to use timber boarding, metal sheeting or some other wall lining. Bear in mind that you don't want to be using gypsum plasterboard in bathrooms at all. Damp and humid conditions in shower areas for example, demand a surface finishing that is unaffected, such as timber or exterior-grade plywood before finishing.

One other benefit of phenolic and urethane insulation boards is that, like most rigid-cellular materials, they resist water vapour penetration and don't normally need any extra vapour barriers. If you are using mineral fibre, it is worth covering it with a thin layer of polythene or foil-backed plasterboard to gain the vapour barrier.

Many materials are now labelled with zero ODP, which stands for ozone depletion potential. CFC/HCFC-free products are also available, particularly with some forms of insulation, and you can rest assured that they are good things to have if you value the upper atmosphere.

Sound insulation
Floors
Unfortunately, the floors in our homes are able to transmit sound efficiently. Wooden joists with chipboard nailed to the top and plasterboard nailed to the bottom make great sounding boards. It doesn't have to be this way – you can, if you want, build in some sound insulation quite cheaply. House developers don't do it because they don't have to, but if you like the idea of having some sound insulation to your loft room, then it really isn't that difficult or expensive to do during the conversion work.

Often, the conversion's structural alterations improve sound insulation anyway without any extra work being done. New floor joists that run alongside the old ceiling joists will isolate the floor from the ceiling reducing the impact sound a bit. Leaving the old insulation between the joists reduces the airborne sound a bit, but bear in mind that thermal insulation is not the same as sound insulation. With sound you are looking for a denser material with less air pockets, and so manufacturers have to produce different materials for the two tasks. If you want to add some real sound insulation, some extra work will be needed.

Once the new floor joists are installed and before the floorboarding is laid, the tops of the joists can be covered by sound-insulation products. Many of these products are simple foam or wool strips, 50 mm wide, that are factory-bonded to pieces of hardboard at intervals. The gaps in between are for stapling the strips down to the joist tops, and the hardboard is for gluing the floor boarding to. Using tongue-

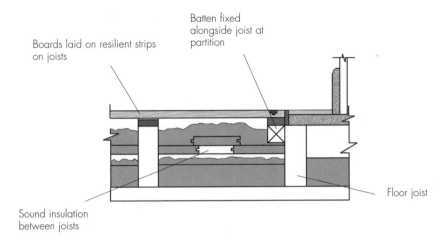

Boards laid on resilient strips on joists

Batten fixed alongside joist at partition

Floor joist

Sound insulation between joists

Sound insulation to floors.

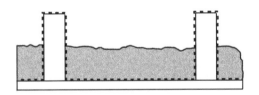

Sound insulation between joists supported by chicken wire.

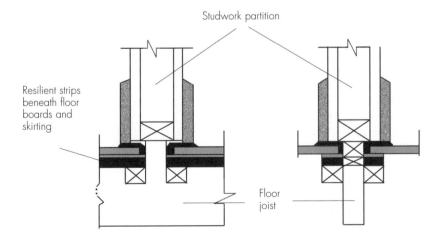

Studwork partition

Resilient strips beneath floor boards and skirting

Floor joist

Sound insulation to floors under studwork partitions.

and-groove chipboard with glued joints for the floating floor finish (no nailing or screwing) will avoid a squeaky floor.

Other types of sound insulation use phenolic foam in sheets that are rolled out over the floor deck and covered again by another layer of floor boarding. These measures deal with impact sound and prevent the things that go bump in the night from resonating through the house below.

To improve on airborne sound insulation, you need to put some mass between the floor joists to absorb it. Traditionally we used sand pugging in bags, but who wants to store sandbags above ceilings these days? Now, mineral fill is more common, which can be a dense mineral-fibre quilt or a pugging of granular minerals. Either way, mass insulation equals weight, and a weight of around 80 kg per sq m can achieve good sound insulation. Those floor joists need to be designed to allow for this kind of weight increase, which in my opinion is best contained within polythene bags suspended by chicken wire over the joists before the impact sound measures are added to the tops of them. Do not rely on the plasterboard ceiling to support the weight of pugging – it isn't designed to.

A loft room floor upgraded by these measures will have a good standard of sound insulation, and should keep you safely in the arms of Morpheus.

Walls

Sound insulation may be necessary if you have a party wall with the converted loft next door. Whether you have enough sound deadening between your new room and theirs will depend on the construction of that separating wall. The chances are it won't be good enough – even with new house building, the standards for sound insulation have been lame over the years, and in roof spaces the standards are reduced as well.

So what can you do to upgrade the wall? Well, you don't have to rebuild it, it can be improved from the surface on your side during the conversion work. The most common method is to build a timber framework using 50 mm x 50 mm square timbers but leaving a gap of at least 25 mm from the wall. This

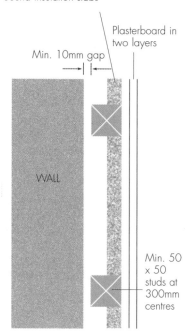

Sound insulation slabs

Plasterboard in two layers

Min. 10mm gap

WALL

Min. 50 x 50 studs at 300mm centres

Sound insulation to a party wall.

air gap is important to prevent the transfer of airborne sound. The framework is then insulated with sound-deadening quilt such as dense mineral fibre. To seal off any air paths through which sound might leak, the gaps around the edges of the frame are filled with acoustic sealant. The framework can then be covered by plasterboard to form a false wall. Yes, you are going to lose about 100 mm off the room by doing this, but the sound insulation benefit should make it worthwhile.

If you have an en-suite bathroom or more than one bedroom proposed, you might choose to provide some sound insulation in the dividing walls. In the past, people have done this by stuffing glass-fibre quilt into the void between the studs of timber partitions. This will help, but thermal quilt isn't dense enough to help much; what is really needed is a suspended sound-deadening quilt continuously hung between the studs, which are fixed off-centre to achieve this. Obviously there is a cost implication in building partitions this way, and you need to weigh that up against the benefits.

Storage space

Ordinarily those short ashlare walls on the sides of your loft room will be somewhere between 800 mm and 1200 mm high – just enough height for a desk, chest of drawers or even a bedhead to sit against (although the risk of whacking your head on the sloping ceiling every morning will stop you from doing the latter), but no good for a wardrobe or anything higher.

Storage in loft rooms tends to have to be low-rise storage, and the easy solution is to use those triangular voids left behind the ashlare walls as storage space. Any number of access doors can be built into these walls, which can be boxed out inside to provide a clean space.

It is worth thinking about the kind of things you want to store here, though. If it needs to be kept at room temperature in dry air, then you should insulate between the rafters right down to the wall plate. If it's just the kind of boxed-up stuff you had in the loft before, then insulate between the ashlare and joists, leaving it as a cold space. If you do this, remember that those hatch doors all need to be lagged on the back with insulation and fitted with draught excluder as well. Last-minute jobs like this are easily forgotten but are important.

If you don't fancy spending so much time on your hands and knees (and I accept that not everybody does), then you can ask your builder to make up some sliding storage bins on runners or wheels that can be pulled out like large drawers. Since these may be harder to insulate, the continuation of the insulation between the rafters will be better for this.

If you don't adopt a sound-proofed floor, the void between the joists could be used. Floor joists in lofts tend to be fairly deep – 200 mm or 225 mm is not uncommon – so with battens between them to support plywood the space could be boxed out for light storage bins here and there. Hinged floor access doors can be laid with recessed handles to sit flush with the floor surface. OK, you are not going to get much in a bin 400 mm wide by 200 mm deep, but it could be quite long ideal for clearing small toys out of the way.

With full height space being at a premium, don't let your designer or builder waste it by placing a door dead-centre in a wall when it could be set to one side, leaving room for a wardrobe. If need be, cut up scaled pieces of card in furniture heights and place them on a cross-section plan to see what can and can't be done. Remember that storage space needs thinking about sooner rather than later if it is to be maximised to its full potential.

The office or study

Loft space makes for an ideal studying or working area. It is naturally isolated from the remainder of your home, with good sound insulation and physical separation. But whether you are converting to form a home office or just a study, you need to give thought to the design of your workspace. The height of desks and shelving may help you decide the height for power points and switches, for example.

Loft plumbing and bathing

Conversion of a loft space solely to provide a bathroom may be unusual, but en-suite bathrooms included with a bedroom are extremely common. For one thing, roof spaces are usually too large for a single bedroom by itself, and providing a new bedroom on a separate storey to the existing bathroom is far from ideal. En-suites are popular these days in first-floor bedrooms, but in second-floor bedrooms they are practically essential. The only question

is where to locate the plumbing.

If you have a conventional heating system with a cold-water tank and expansion tank in the loft, then you are going to have to find some room up there somewhere to relocate them. Coffin tanks may be the answer; as their name suggests, they are long and thin and not as deep as conventional tanks, enabling them to be squeezed into confined spaces. If you have just a tiny loft space left below the ridge, then you may be able to get a coffin tank in here above the ceiling ties.

Make sure your designers have allowed for this. A standard cold water tank is heavy when full (about a quarter of a tonne), and those short ceiling joists (collars) are usually just fixed to the rafters. If they haven't been designed in from the start, they will sag and possibly collapse.

Combi boilers

Making life so much easier for the loft converter is the combination boiler, which requires no water tanks to be left in the loft, or indeed anywhere. Combi boilers produce instantaneous hot water to the taps and to the central heating system without the need to store water in cylinders or tanks at all – ideal for loft conversions, and if you haven't got one at the moment you could do a lot worse than to replace your existing boiler with one as part of the work.

Combi boilers have come down in price since the new century began, they are much more compact than they used to be, and are easier to install and generally less complex now. In the very long term, they will save you money on your fuel bill, particularly condensing combi boilers, which operate at a higher efficiency (they don't waste so much heat) as standard boilers. Not only that, but they can be installed with balanced flues just about anywhere in the house where you can get water to. And that includes lofts.

Some combi boilers possess a built-in hot water vessel that can store up to 7 or 8 l of hot water and deliver it to the taps instantly at a rate of up to 13 or 14 l per minute. They don't work so well if you have several bathrooms and showers because they simply can't keep up with the demand if they are all used at the same time, but otherwise they are an excellent upgrade to make.

Condensing boilers

Condensing boilers are said to have efficiencies of up to 95 per cent compared to a ten-year-old conventional boiler that may be running around 65–70 per cent efficient, efficiency being measured by how little of the produced heat is going to waste through the flue pipe, etc.

Condensing boilers have large heat exchangers that condense flue gases, adding latent heat back to the boiler. The side effect of this process is the water vapour has to be released externally through a water pipe, and therefore the siting of the boiler has to be given some extra consideration, i.e. not above doors or windows, where the water may scald you.

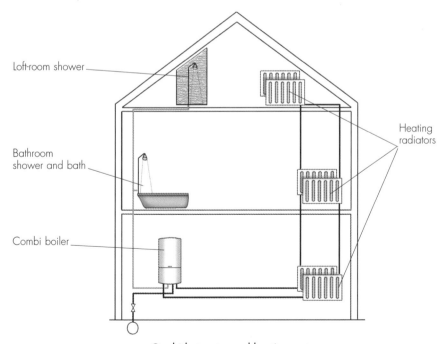

Loft-room shower

Bathroom shower and bath

Combi boiler

Heating radiators

Combi hot water and heating system.

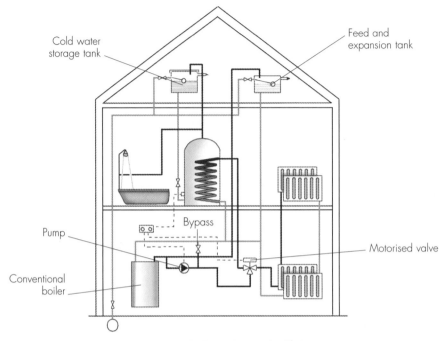

Conventional boiler with vented cylinder

Combi-condensing boilers are considered the most efficient, space-saving and therefore popular. Every so often energy-efficiency grants or schemes appear to promote reduced energy use in our homes, and often they offer cash-back incentives for changing to such a boiler.

Interior design and sanitaryware

Bathrooms in the UK have seen some interesting fashions over the years – in the 1970s we were washing in avocado and burgundy bathroom suites with mirror tiles before the 1980s brought pastel shades with them. Now I've lost track of where we are in the fashion

cycle when it comes to colours. Black and white with chrome accessories has become popular, a bit like you'd expect to see in the toilets of a modern stylish hotel or health club. Sanitaryware (I hate that word) is definitely white again, and anything Victorian with feet on is always popular. If it stands in the middle of the room and looks like the floor has had to be strengthened beneath it, it's in vogue.

Glass basins with chrome traps seem to have flooded the designer bathroom market, and although I have no problem with this extended to baths, I hope they draw the line at WC pans.

If you decide on a pumped shower to boost water pressure, then I would recommend locating the pump on its own stand in the void somewhere, where it can sit on its anti-vibration feet and hum as much as it likes without resonating through the house.

The choice in bathroom appliances has grown dramatically in recent years, with the advent of spa baths and massaging showers. Even materials for basic appliances are variable from acrylic to steel. Acrylic itself comes in many thicknesses and hence with variable durability, and you should always bear in mind that you are basically going to get what you pay for when it comes to quality. The powder-coated steel baths are cheap but much stronger than the cheap fibreglass models – you just need to remember to run the hot water before the cold, as it will warm the steel before you climb in.

The latest in contemporary WC appliances hang off the wall and don't sit on the floor at all; instead they seem to just hover above it, and this means less complication for the carpet fitter. It also makes the room look bigger because the floor is uncluttered. I like the look of them, but frankly wall-hung toilets scare me. Is there a weight limit? Is it OK to swing your feet? I don't know, but it must take some getting used to, just to overcome the feeling that you are sitting on a shelf bracket.

Decorating your loft room

Wall colours tend to be bold at present and create a definite temperature in the bathroom. Anything goes with a white suite, and insurance claims must be reduced because of that – no longer will it be necessary to change the entire suite when you break the toilet cistern lid, because the colour is out of line.

Daylight saturation from loft windows becomes a bit of a drawback now. UV light will cause wallpapers and upholstery to fade. So before you pick out the colours and the furniture for your new room, give some thought to protecting them with blinds to the windows.

Rooflight blinds are expensive, at least the ones sold by the rooflight manufacturers are. They do an essential job, however, of keeping your loft room cool in the summer from the burning sun and filtering the UV light down to harmless levels. You can have your windows glazed with special glass that cuts out ultraviolet rays, but there is a cost implication of course.

Depending on the use of your room, you have the choice of either filtering down the sunlight or blacking it out. I know these blinds are designed to fit the windows precisely and be easy to operate, but I have a condition that prevents me from handling those tiny strings without getting them twisted and caught. It also means that I can't lower both sides of a blind simultan-eously or slowly, but can only drop half of it suddenly and then not get it back up again. The science involved in making them is well beyond my grasp, and unless you have been trained as a puppeteer I can't see how you can possibly work them.

If I'm not alone in this condition – and I accept that I might be – about the only alternative aside from the electrical-powered blinds is to rig up some curtains like sailcloths suspended

10 Expert Points

HERE ARE TEN POINTS TO BEAR IN MIND WHEN CONVERTING YOUR ROOF TO WORK FROM HOME:

1 POWER POINTS

Don't underestimate the number of socket outlets you require, and choose double sockets over single ones. The cost difference is negligible since the labour element is identical and the materials difference insignificant. Running just one computer station these days with a printer and scanner will mean six sockets, so three doubles should be the minimum you look for at a workstation. Desktop lights, fax machines, photocopiers, music systems etc. will add to that.

2 COMPUTERS

I am told that IT equipment leaks current to earth by design, so if you are installing plenty of it your electrician may need to provide for high earth leakage over currents.

3 TELEPHONE POINTS

With telephone points needed not just for phones but modems and fax machines, rather than run extensions leads everywhere it would be best to have another separate line installed. This must be a good idea anyway if you have a PC with an Internet connection or FAX machine, since you'll be able to use it and the phone at the same time. I just hope that one day phone companies will provide some kind of line-rental discount for those homes with more than one line, and make it more affordable. If you do run extension leads, at least conceal the cabling in service ducts so it is out of sight and not a trip hazard.

4 ELECTRICAL CABLES

If the ashlare walls of your loft room are lagged with glass-fibre insulation, you need to ensure that it doesn't surround the electrical cables without them being rated accordingly. Cable rating is halved by doing this to counteract the risk of it overheating, hence for a 15-amp circuit, a cable rated at 30 amps must be used.

5 PLANNING THE ELECTRICAL LAYOUT

There are no special requirements contained within the IEE wiring regulations for loft conversions, but the installation as a whole should comply, as with any other electrical work. It may be necessary for your electrician to install a new ring circuit for the loft run from and back to the distribution board; alternatively, if the floor space limits allow, the ring circuit of the floor below may be extended. Obviously you will want your electrician to do this connection wiring through concealed parts of the structure, and not through chased conduits cut into the wall plaster or surface conduits. The same goes for the cables linking smoke detectors – it is important that the electrical first fix takes place as a planned exercise once the structural work is done if you are to avoid having surface conduit running up your walls at the end of the job. Make sure you know what you want in the way of power points, lighting and switching well in advance, and if your designers hasn't marked the plans with them, mark out a copy yourself for the electrician to work to.

6 DESKTOPS

An ideal desktop height is 700 mm, but remember that you won't be able to reach files on shelves much higher than 450 mm above the desktop without standing.

7 CUPBOARD SPACE AND SHELVING

Rather than try to fit standard filing cabinets and shelves to the room, purpose-made built cabinets and shelving will achieve a far superior use of space. You can also make sure that shelves are strong enough, of the right height for your files and books, and secured to strengthened parts of the walls. Plywood or MDF boards screwed direct to the structure as lining panels for shelves and cupboards will be far stronger than plasterboard, which has limits for fixings and is prone to impact damage.

8 ISDN

If you are really hot-desking (being paid to work from home, and nothing to do with earthing electrics to metal furniture) from your office, then you may be thinking about installing an ISDN link with your head office. You can run your service cables behind PVC-U skirting boards that are specifically designed for the office, with separated channels behind the face.

9 AIR CIRCULATION

Avoid draughts from doors or window vents at low level – when working at a desk for long periods of a time, your feet need to stay warm. Radiators are best placed beneath windows so that the warm air rising from them reduces surface condensation on the glazing, mixes with the cool air and circulates it back into the room. Shelves or wide window cills above radiators are to be avoided. Most skylights have a crack ventilation opening that allows them to be locked fractionally open to provide a supply of background ventilation.

10 HUMIDITY AND HEALTH

For most of the time we aim to provide a dry, warm atmosphere in our homes. It's good for the structure. But not so good for us – sore eyes, dry skin and throats abound in our centrally heated worlds, and in a workspace charged with electrical appliances the effects on our health can be worsened. In your own office you have nobody to blame but yourself. Introduce some large-leafed plants – banana plants are ideal – and an indoor water feature that will help to humidify and balance the air quality. Desk lights can be fitted with daylight simulation bulbs, PC monitors placed in shaded areas away from glare, etc. In short, think about your health and comfort while you work.

between two poles, top and bottom. It makes for a touch of romance, and is less stressful.

When you decorate, think of colours that will warm the room. Colours that react well with direct sunshine are yellows and reds – tones that hold in some of that warmth and make you feel good about being up there.

If you have installed an en-suite bath or shower room, you might want to create an image of freshness and cleanliness in there with a lighter tone that reflects the light. This has the added bonus of making the room appear more spacious than it actually is.

I hope I haven't put you off. Sitting in your loft room in early spring or late autumn, warming yourself in a pool of sunlight, will be a pleasure beyond measure. Vitamin D will flood your bones, and when everybody else is edging on SAD syndrome you'll be as cheerful as a lark. I envy you.

CHAPTER 5

Basements

The low life

Basements can make ideal rooms: they are soundproofed from external noise and free from the dramatic changes in temperature that lofts suffer from. Providing you can introduce sufficient daylight and ventilation, cellar space long since abandoned or used only for storing wine, can become part of your home. Consistently cool, cellars make for ideal kitchens and playrooms – and heated and opened up, they can be used to extend living room space.

As with loft conversions, they can present you with restricted headroom, but with basements you have the added possibility of lowering the floor a little.

Before embarking on a basement conversion it is important to understand how the space relates to the structure of your home and the ground outside it. Victorian houses were commonly built with cellars beneath the timber ground floors to store coal for the fires, but often these cellars did not extend to the full width of the property, and some do not have the benefit of an external wall, let alone a window. An interior basement like this is best converted by opening it up to another room on the ground floor, in effect creating a split-level open-plan arrangement. By doing so, the below-ground space can benefit from the daylight and ventilation of the ground level room above. By just how much you enlarge the stairwell opening to achieve this will depend on the layout of your house and the position of the existing windows. Obviously it will be a matter of balancing the loss of some ground floor space against the need for light and air in the new room below, but this type of layout can add interest and value to your home. In addition to this, you have avoided the creation of an 'inner room' and the fire safety risk that that raises.

Of course some basements may already have windows and light-wells formed, and this will widen the options open to you for the room's use. If your basement has a decent window you will probably want to convert it as a separate room. Before deciding on the position of the staircase, take a look at the opening size of the window and see whether it can be utilised or replaced to form an opening big enough to climb out through (a minimum of a 500 mm wide by 850 mm high opening is ideal). With a window considered large enough to double as an emergency exit, you are able to position the basement staircase, if you want, within an existing room above, rendering the basement space as an inner room. A suitable window like this can be locked securely, but with a quick-release catch rather than a key lock. It will expand the range of uses of the basement to include bedrooms.

If you have the possibility of installing a new window, then seize it, but if it just isn't possible, seek to position the stairs in the hallway or lobby of the ground floor. As with loft conversions, the installation of a mains-wired smoke alarm interlinked with one on the floor above will be a valuable asset, giving you early warning in the event of a fire.

Max. 100 mm gap

Stair with enclosed risers (left) and stair with half-risers (right).

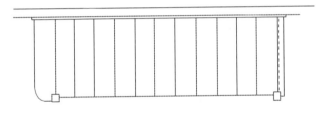

Straight staircase.

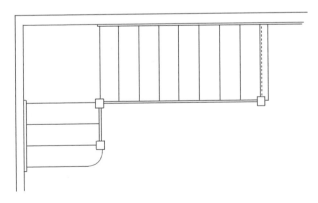

Stair with quarter-turn landing and bullnose tread.

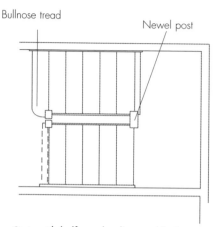

Bullnose tread

Newel post

Stair with half-turn landing and bullnose tread.

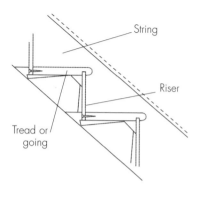

String

Riser

Tread or going

Section through stairs.

Room use and layout

Arranging the layout of rooms so that they make sense to the way you use your home not only makes life easier for you, it makes the place more marketable and valuable if you ever decide to sell or rent it. This might sound like common sense, but you would be surprised how many people don't think about the layout – creating bedrooms that can only be accessed by passing through another room is a common mistake.

But certain rooms are related and can be accessed from each other. Basement playrooms, entertainment rooms and dining rooms could, for example, be accessed from a lounge above, or en-suite bathrooms from bedrooms, utility rooms from kitchens, and so on.

For a habitable room, daylight should be provided by windows sized to at least 10 per cent of the floor area

they serve, but with basements that rely upon light-wells, illumination is greatly reduced. The décor you choose can be used to help reflect the light around to compensate this fact. White painted walls are ideal.

For adequate ventilation, window openings should be equal to at least 5% of the floor area and fitted with background or trickle vents. If you're planning on using the space for a kitchen, utility room or bathroom, then you will need to have an extractor fan installed to remove the condensation more rapidly. It will be a case of mounting it on the ceiling and running the duct between the joists and through the wall to the outside air.

Floors

Retaining the existing floor

Is the floor level? Check it in several positions with a 1.2 m long spirit level or straight edge. A brick cellar floor could be left rustic and uneven if you aren't planning on fitting floor cupboards, for example – adjustable feet on some kitchen units will only take so much adjustment!

The surface could be cleaned and painted with a clear silicone water sealant to finish it.

Assuming you are fortunate enough to have a sound existing floor but you're looking towards achieving a totally level finish, a product known as levelling compound is ideal for overcoming small discrepancies in level and is floated on as a slurry-like mix. If the levels are too far out, then it will need to be screeded with a mixture of cement and sand in a 1 to 3 parts ratio. Before this can be done, however, the concrete floor should be cleaned and treated with three coats of liquid- bitumen-based damp-proof membrane. This will ensure that the floor finish remains free from damp.

If you can spare the headroom you should take this opportunity to install a layer of floor-grade insulation before screeding, but check to make sure that the screed thickness applied is at least

65 mm floating screed with mesh

Concrete floor slab

Insulation cut and placed vertically at perimeter

Polythene separating layer/vapour control layer

Damp-proof membrane

Sand blinding on hardcore

Ground floor slab.

65 mm. Any less and the screed will crack later.

New floors

It is unlikely that the existing basement floor is resistant to damp or insulated against heat loss. It may not even be

OVERSITE MATERIAL	
USE	**AVOID**
Clean broken bricks, concrete, tiles ONLY for hardcore	Colliery shale
	Soft Insulating broken blocks
Reject or crushed stone (washed)	Poor-quality demolition rubble
Type 1 or Type 2 graded stone	Road scrapings

10 Expert Points

THE FOLLOWING TEN POINTS WILL HELP YOU TO ENSURE A GOOD REPLACEMENT FLOOR:

1 FORMATION LEVEL
Ensure that the existing floor is totally broken up and topsoil removed, and begin from your calculated formation level.

2 MATERIAL
Ensure you use acceptable material for hardcore (see the table on page 106).

3 MATERIAL SIZE
Ensure the hardcore material is no greater sized than 100 mm (half-brick) units.

4 LEVELS
Ensure that you have correctly calculated the depth of construction through to finished floor level and that your oversite 'finished' level is correct. Mark the level on the walls before filling.

5 DEPTH OF FILL
Ensure this covers at least 150 mm in thickness. Ensure that the hardcore, if deeper than 150 mm, does not exceed 600 mm in total thickness. Where part of the make-up may exceed 600 mm deep, it may be acceptable to use lean-mix concrete in layers, and use the hardcore to make up the difference.

6 COMPACTION
Ensure that the hardcore is compacted in layers no more than 225 mm thick and ideally mechanically compacted with a plate compactor, but take care not to push out the external walls where a stone-type fill is used.

7 BLINDING
Ensure it is blinded with fine material such as sand to a maximum thickness of 20 mm. Do not lay the blinding material too thick. It is only intended to protect the polythene DPM from being punctured by sharp edges of hardcore.

8 DPM
Lap and tape down polythene if it is cut for the DPM (damp-proof membrane). Ensure the DPM is dressed up the outside walls so it can be trimmed back after concreting. The DPM can help to protect the concrete slab from sulphate attack. Sulphates may be contained in some fill material, such as brick rubble.

9 INSULATION
Use the correct depth and type of insulation graded for floors, not walls! Expanded polystyrene is often used in 50 mm thickness. Cut the insulation into strips and stand it up the sides of walls to the slab depth when insulating below the concrete slab so that the slab is fully encased. Whilst floor grade insulation can be laid beneath the concrete, there are advantages in it being placed later on top of the concrete beneath the finishings.

10 CRACK AVOIDANCE
Make sure you are not forming the hardcore on filled or contaminated ground, or where subsoil shrinkage or heave will cause problems. Even on good subsoil, the addition of lightweight fabric reinforcement such as A142 is beneficial to avoiding settlement cracks.

In very large basements movement joints such as fibrous material strips should be used to allow some expansion to occur without damaging the slab.

particularly level, and so most conversion work will include the construction of a new solid floor. If you are short of headroom, there is the possibility that you can break up the existing floor, dig out a little and reform it lower, but great care should be taken not to extend the digging below the wall foundations. Small trial holes can be dug to check their depth before starting.

- There are sound environmental reasons for reusing demolition hardcore in oversite preparations, but it is essential that it is hand-picked and 'clean'. Be prepared to spend some time sifting the rubbish out.

- Sulphates in hardcore or in subsoil can attack concrete. Use sulphate-resisting cement in lieu of ordinary Portland cement. Polythene DPMs also helps to resist sulphate attack.

- This preparation is subject to a one-day 'statutory notice' of inspection to the Building Control Surveyor, who will need to inspect the work before the concrete is poured.

It is not often possible to include a suspended timber floor in a basement conversion, since such floors need to be served by good ventilation from the outside air. If you are set on the warm feel of a timber floor compared to a solid one, you could choose a floating floor finish where tongue-and-groove floorboards or chipboard sheets are laid over the insulation instead of screed.

DIY CONCRETE MIX FOR GROUND-BEARING SLABS

25 kg (0.0175 cu m) of cement to

0.05 cu m of building sand to

0.1 cu m of coarse aggregate.

(or ten (x 25 kg) bags of cement to every cubic metre of all-in ballast)

Checks for floating floors

- Ensure that the insulation is laid perfectly flat and level on the concrete slab. To achieve this, the slab will need a trowelled finish or to be surfaced with levelling compound.

- A thin polythene vapour barrier can be laid over the insulation before the boarding is laid.

- The joints between boards should all be glued and the skirting pinning down the floorboards at the edges.

- A 10 mm expansion gap should exist at the perimeter, which the skirting and wall finish will later hide.

Walls

Tanking

Of course it is not only the floor that will need damp-proofing down here, the walls will do as well. Remember that you are below DPC and ground level, so there is no point in a chemical-injection DPC being applied to them. In a conversion such as this, you have to accept the fact that the walls themselves may always be damp and concentrate on ensuring that the damp doesn't get through to the inside surfaces.

Damp-proofing a whole wall like this is called 'tanking', and it is arguably the most important element of the conversion. Of course, it may also be necessary to tank internal walls if they are built attached to the external ones, allowing damp to penetrate through, or if they have no DPC at floor level.

There are a variety of methods and materials for tanking, and specialist advice should be sought to establish which one is best for you. The choice will depend a great deal on the condition of the walls and the extent of dampness that exists. Traditionally it was done with asphalt, but this is seldom used today. Bitumen-based products that can be applied in self-adhesive sheets or painted on (with a broom) to set as a rubber latex seal are more popular. The drawback with these is that they usually require the wall to be dry and primed before they are applied, otherwise they simply won't stick to the surface.

If you have a wet wall that is subject to active ground-water pressure, then bitumen won't be suitable and you will have to look towards one of the dimpled semi-rigid sheet membranes that allow the water to flow behind them safely, or address the problem from the outside with land drainage.

Whichever method you select, the damp-proofing treatment to the walls should be compatible and married to that used in the floor to achieve a continuous seal, if your new room is to remain dry. Most damp-proofing products come with guarantees if they are applied in accordance with the manufacturer's instructions, so obtain a copy from the supplier and see that they are followed.

Drainage cavity system of waterproofing

With this method of tanking all of the work is again carried out from the inside, making it ideal for treating existing basements in conversion. The walls and floors are lined with a continuous sheet membrane that is fixed in place but creates a cavity space of air behind it – not a huge space of air, but an important space none the less. It achieves this by being corrugated or dimpled in profile and of a semi-rigid nature, a type of plastic and impervious to water. This cavity allows the walls and floor to breathe and provides a drainage channel through which water coming through them can be diverted without it penetrating through to the internal finishings of the room.

As you can imagine, these products are specialised and require their own fixings to secure them to the walls – a kind of masonry plug with a seal to ensure the waterproofing isn't compromised. After that, plasterboard

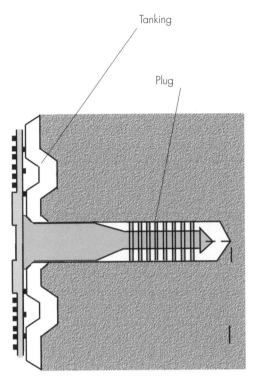

Tanking

Plug

Tanking retaining plug.

can be erected as dry-lining, often supported on channels or brackets that are independent from the membrane. In some systems, one face of the membrane is fibreglass mesh finished to provide a key that can be wet-plastered directly to if you prefer.

If you do adopt this option, you need to be aware that you can never drill a hole in the wall to hang a picture – and so do any future occupants of the property. Since this might prove a trifle difficult, I would recommend that you forsake the hard plaster finish and opt for dry-lining. You will always be able to use plasterboard plugs for fixing things.

Dry-lining the walls has one further benefit that is essential if you are heating your new basement – insulation. You can insulate behind the plasterboard with a rigid mineral-fibre insulation batten or a high-performing polyurethane foam board, or you choose a plasterboard already bonded with insulation, a laminated board. Your choice of insulation really is only governed by the price and how well insulated you want the basement to be. Naturally, with the walls being below ground it will have some natural insulation that those above don't have, but there is plenty of scope for

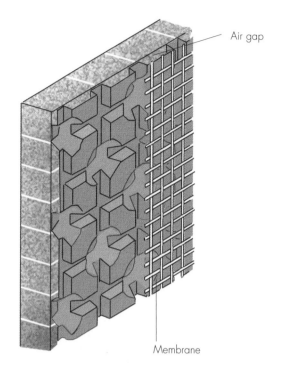

Air gap

Membrane

Drainage cavity tanking.

upgrading its thermal resistance and making it energy-efficient space.

With the floor membrane needing no fixing at all, an insulation board can be laid over the top and the floor finished with either screed or timber boarding simply floated (not nailed) in position. Floating timber floors are only retained by glued tongue-and grooved-joints and the skirting board around the edges.

In a basement that has a unhealthy amount of damp in the floor and the walls, this drained cavity method of tanking is perhaps the most reliable, but if your cellar suffers from flooding with active water penetration during the winter months it will still work, providing you take the system one step further. The water behind the membrane must be kept on the move – if it does this by naturally flowing from one side of the basement to another via this continuous cavity then fine, but the chances are it just comes in everywhere and fills the cavity up, unless you create a drainage channel around the perimeter of the floor that collects the water draining down the walls and coming up through the floor and takes it to a sump, from which it is pumped out and into the drains outside your house. In a basement that floods reliably every winter this may be the only guaranteed way of keeping it dry, drastic as this may sound.

Sometimes trying to keep water out of a cellar by trying to physically hold it back is a bit like King Canute trying to hold back the tide. Ground water pressure is often exceptional, and if you can resist the urge to try and stop it and think more about diverting it around your home, either internally as described above or externally with land drains, then you are in with a good chance of success.

Polyurethane resin tanking

This is a liquid tanking method that is applied by spray, brush or roller to the walls. After two days the material has dried out to form a surface that remains flexible but fully bonded to the wall and waterproof.

Land drainage

Sometimes known as French drains, land drains are essentially free-draining channels created around buildings to divert water away from them. Today they are always accompanied by irrigation pipes laid in the bottom to collect the water and channel it convincingly to somewhere else. Perforated pipes are drainage pipes with holes or slots cut in them that allow the water to filter in.

Some care needs to be taken here to check the correct type is used because there are two different sorts. You are going to need the type with holes or slots in the top of the pipe, but not in the bottom since you want to collect water coming down through the

drainage material and have it run away from the building.

The other type has holes or slots all the way around, and is often flexible like ducting. This type is ideal for irrigation such as with septic tank drainage or horticultural uses where you actually want the water to drain through and disperse into the ground beneath the pipe, the very thing you are trying to avoid here. Land drains that are carefully constructed can be highly effective, but so often they are poorly formed and of limited use.

Ideally the excavated trench should be lined with a geotextile material that permits water penetration but prevents earth washing in that in time would cause the drain to silt up. If you've taken the trouble to excavate a land drain alongside your basement's external wall, you might as well provide a waterproof barrier against the wall before completing the drain. Dealing with the water on the positive face is without a doubt the best place to do it – in fact, some products on the market only work in positive pressure like this, where they are supported by the ground and the water pressure against them.

What are your options for damp-proofing the outside of the wall? If you are still proposing to tank the basement internally, then anything you do out here is a bonus and 1200-gauge polythene is as effective as anything and cheap. The sheet will need lapping at the joints and taping the joints with the DPM duct tape available for this purpose, but it shouldn't be fixed to the wall. Simply let it hang down the face from batten fixed to the wall above ground level where it will be cut off later, and backfill the drain.

It is important to use a round stone backfill rather than a crushed stone with sharp edges that could easily puncture the DPM. You need to use anything from 10 mm up in granular size and something that is non-cohesive and free-draining to create an effective French drain. If you are aiming to deal with the problem of waterproofing totally from the outside – and there are products available that suggest you can – then you will need to excavate a wider trench that you can work in, because these products require the wall to be thoroughly cleaned off and dry before they are applied. This is definitely a job for a dry season. Most of the materials available for this are bitumen-based and form a thicker seal than polythene, but they do require supporting if they are going to be able to work properly.

First, the wall will undoubtedly have to treated with a bitumen-based primer once it is clean and dry to provide a key for the DPM. Second, the DPM itself, which may come in the form of a self-adhesive sheet on a roll, or a liquid paint-on solution, will require careful application. Some of the newest forms available are torch-applied, and the best person for such a job is a flat-roofing contractor who will possess the necessary skills and equipment.

Once the DPM is bonded to the wall (and not peeling away from it as you stand there), a protection board can be placed against it before the trench is backfilled. Be warned that some of these products go one step further by suggesting that a masonry wall be used before backfilling with a cavity filled with dry sand or mortar packed down to support the DPM as the wall is built. This is a specification that can be used in new basement construction and done from the inside (in reverse), where it relies upon integration with DPCs built into the wall – and where the supporting masonry leaf can be built up off of the foundation or floor structure. You might not have an existing foundation wide enough to allow this, so be careful about proceeding with this method if you are unsure it will work.

Manufacturers of damp-proofing and tanking will advise on the best way of using their own products and will often supply sketch diagrams and specifications for the work free of charge, so use them.

Drainage channels like these are designed to be covered over, flush to the finishing floor but with built-in service points that allow the channels to be cleaned out when they become silted up. In this respect, they have the advantage over external land drains.

The weakest point of a basement, from a damp-penetration point of view, is usually the edges of the floor abutting the external walls, so these channels are located in the best position to relieve that water pressure and maintain a dry basement.

If your basement is already tanked but damp is still appearing at these abutments, then the installation of one of these proprietary drainage systems may be all that is required to resolve the problem, without any further waterproofing treatments being required at all.

The winter of 2000/2001 was one of the wettest since records began, and many properties were flooded throughout the country. Basements are the first to suffer in conditions where ground water is rising, and unfortunately many of them are poorly constructed or converted, able to resist damp with conventional tanking methods but wholly incapable of resisting water pressure.

Where a river bursts its banks and flows down the High Street, nothing is going to help, aside from an inflatable boat, but where rising ground water is concerned, a pumped drainage system is everything you need to keep dry until it drops to its normal level.

If you don't like the idea or the cost of a plastic studded drainage membrane, or you believe your cellar to be relatively dry, you might want to consider a wet-application system of waterproof cement. This is normally applied in coats like plaster with a trowel, or sometimes a brush or spraygun. You can't use these systems where the walls are contaminated with sulphates (salts).

Tanking of this kind is aimed at sealing the walls and floor against damp penetration, with cement-based plaster containing plastic additives creating an impervious barrier. One of the side effects of such a system is that the stuff does tend to seal up any hairline cracks or gaps in the structure.

All basements allude to dampness, but in some cases it may be just down to condensation, and once they are insulated, heated and ventilated, their environment will be transformed.

The dry basement

There are people in this country who live in areas where the ground water table never rises, where the subsoil is stony or rocky, solid chalk even, for goodness sake, and where the words 'groundwater' or 'rising damp' have the locals reaching for a dictionary. They are in the high country far from rivers, lakes and the coast, and even global warming won't bother them.

If you are one of those people and you have a basement that – by some awful neglect – has yet to be properly used, then you are probably wondering if you need to invest in any damp-proofing at all. Quite possibly not, but if you are planning on insulating or lining the walls in any way, then you should include damp-proofing to protect those linings.

In these situations a liquid brush-on damp-proofing product is likely to be sufficient. These products are sometimes bitumen-based and are applied in two or three coats before the surface finishes can be formed. More advanced ones are epoxy-resin in nature with a base coat and a hardener that sets to a tough abrasion-resistant finish. Again the wall has got to be dry and dust-free, but with theses types it shouldn't need priming. Brush- or roller-applied, it takes a day for each coat to dry, and if you want to render or plaster the wall direct, you will need to dress the final coat with some fine aggregate before the plaster fully sets, to get a key.

I think that sometimes the expectation for existing basement walls to be in excellent condition is asking too much for these products to be used trouble-free, but they do even suggest that sharp edges in the bricks may cause problems. Clearly a stone or flintwork wall is not going to be okay for liquid treatments.

I don't believe that skilled labour is needed for this work. Liquid tanking can be applied with a decorator's roller or bristle brush by anyone who can read the manufacturers' instructions. The only thing is, you will need a well-ventilated basement because the stuff gives off some nasty fumes – either that, or you will have to work with a respirator. Be prepared to throw away your protective gloves and clothing afterwards as well, because these products are tar-like in nature and can't be cleaned out.

British Standard 8102:1990 gives advice in considerable detail on the damp treatment of basements, and you may wish to include a reference to it in your specification to builders.

One final word on tanking basements. It is only necessary for the tanking to extend 150 mm above the outside ground level. In other words, don't be fooled into thinking that the entire height of the basement walls need to be done if only half of it is below ground level.

Contamination

If you suspect that your basement is suffering from contamination leaching in through the walls or floor, it is important to determine the nature of it before you can start with any tanking or damp-proofing work.

Undoubtedly it will need to be dealt with before tanking applications can begin. Basement floors themselves may contain contamination within the old hardcore or concrete perhaps, or from oil or coal if once used as a fuel store. All of the contaminated material should be carefully removed before proceeding. Your Environmental Health Department may be able to give you some advice on the nature of the contamination, or you may have to engage the services of an environmental consultant if you are unsure about the nature of it or how to remove it safely.

Not all forms of contamination are visible, or smellable, come to that. Methane gas can migrate from nearby landfill sites, permeating the soil and leaking into basements through the structure. If you are within 500 m of a landfill site or known methane contaminated area, you should have your basement checked for methane-contamination. Methane can build up in basements to a potentially dangerous level, but it is easily dealt with. By installing with your tanking a methane-resistant material, the room can be sealed against any further infiltration of the gas. Many self-adhesive sheet damp-proof membranes also come in gas-resistant form with an aluminium layer incorporated in the sheet.

Another form of gas contamination is radon. This gas, however, is natural, occurring in certain geological conditions (granite, to be specific) and hence is prevalent to those areas where that bedrock occurs. Again, basements are at risk from radon, which can build up in them, putting your health at risk. As with methane, gas-resistant membranes can be incorporated in the tanking of the walls and floors to seal against the gas. Any services entering the building from the outside will need sealing around too. Quite often with basements in radon-affected areas continuous ventilation is essential to guard against gas build-up.

You can find out if you are in a radon-risk area by contacting your local Environmental Health Department. An atlas, or more likely a GIS mapping system held by your local authority, should contain a record of where known contamination exists. Under the Environmental Protection Act, local authorities have a duty to make information more available to the public. In years gone by, landfill atlases produced by local government waste-management divisions were maintained confidentially and were not available to public view, but in these enlightened times we have come to accept that contamination is better identified and dealt with to ensure that we live in a healthy environment.

Fixtures and fittings

Invariably basements, like loft rooms, are small and space is at a premium, but with basements you have the luxury of continuous headroom across the whole floor. The difficulty is that if you're looking to build in cupboards and storage units in basements, they will make the room look even smaller. In a loft they can look good fitted into the low spaces beneath the sloping roof, but here they will bring a full-height wall forward.

One trick of creating the look of space is to keep units off the floor down here. If you can't secure them to the wall with heavy duty fixings because of the tanking, then consider hanging them from the floor joists above. Your carpenter should be able to build something that will be suspended from several joists to spread the load; together with the point of the load being close to the joist's end bearings at the wall, the supporting floor will be more than sufficient for most storage. Ideally the units should have purpose-made brackets that are side-fixed to the cabinets and the joists with screws, rather than rely solely on screwing up into the joist bottoms. Fixing to the sides means that the weight is taken by the sheer strength of the steel screw in the timber, rather than its weaker withdrawal strength. Now tell me that a TV makeover show would suggest that.

Even kitchen units which are raised up on adjustable feet can be left with the bottom plinth off and low-voltage lighting installed to reveal the floor beneath. This gives them the illusion of almost hovering on the light, and creates the deception of more space.

Never underestimate the value of glass fixtures and fittings. You might not be able to run to a full glass kitchen, but if you need a dining table or even a coffee table in your basement room, a glass one won't steal the floor space away. Glass display cabinets lit by built-in cabinet lights can themselves shed enough light to illuminate the room for meals or relaxing.

Even sound system speakers can be fitted flush to the ceiling, with the cables built in between the joists. This takes away the box speakers that we have always been forced to stand in the corners by the standard lamp and Yucca plant. The latest TVs available don't just have a flat screen but a flat tube, ultra-slim models that can be supported on the wall like pictures, and these – when they come down in price – are bound to become standard items. The corners of our rooms will never look the same again.

Electrical installations

In wiring up a basement, the best you can hope for is a separate circuit run from a spare fuseway on your existing fuseboard. Two would be even better – one for the power ring-main and one for the new lighting circuit. Ask your electrician to label up the fuseboard with a key that tells you which fuses or MCBs control which parts of the house, if it hasn't been done already. It will make life so much easier when you are doing maintenance in the future. If there are no spare fuseways, your electrician may be able to install a separate new fuse unit. If the board itself just isn't that accessible for a new circuit, then the existing circuits supplying the ground floor may be extendable, perhaps.

Perhaps the drawback for these options lies more on the lighting side with the circuit extended from the floor above. If it controls the lights in the rooms directly above the basement, the hall or whatever you use to access the room, and the fuse blows you are

going to be plunged into darkness right throughout your exit. If possible, ask the electrician to stagger the lighting circuits so power isn't removed from complete routes out of the house. One tripped or fused circuit needn't be such a problem then.

Lighting

Good lighting doesn't have to be bright and even, unless you expressly want it that way. It can be subdued or creatively focused and add a whole new dimension to your basement room.

As with loft conversions, basements can suffer from low ceilings, making them difficult to light with normal pendant fittings, but ideal for recessed ceiling or wall lighting.

I have seen so much recessed ceiling lighting lately that I wonder if I might be going off it. Recessed lighting is diverse, but you would never think so. It can be mains-voltage or low-voltage, halogen or spot lamps, beam-focused or beam-spread and so on. You could choose to fit a narrow-beam low-voltage light directly over a favourite reading chair, or a wide-beam spotlight across a table.

Once upon a time only shopfitters wiring up fashion stores peppered the ceiling with low-voltage halogen lamps, but the trend extended to homes at the end of the twentieth century and caught on big-time – not always with the greatest of care, either. This is a shame really, because there is so much creativity to be enjoyed with lighting, and basements can be the perfect place to exercise it.

If your basement is fortunate enough to have a vaulted ceiling, or if you've designed two different wall finishes, then it is worth giving a lot of thought to how best they can be illuminated with wall lamps.

White light is unbeatable, particularly when it is focused on relatively small areas with little fall-off around the edges. Alternate uplighters and downlighters along a wall or on opposing walls can create a novel effect. Wherever you can, look to conceal the light source itself unless it is an architectural showpiece itself. Uplighters by themselves create an even, reflected light, free from glare.

Look around for good ideas, visit public buildings and generally try to get some ideas for how you want your basement room to feel. Best of all, if you can find reputable electricians who have some experience of creative or even theatrical lighting, they will undoubtedly be able to furnish you with plenty of ideas.

Introducing coloured lamps into the home is very much a matter of personal taste. Crisp white lights from halogen lamps are the in thing, but coloured dichroic lamps are now available, giving purer colour saturation than the old coloured-glass bulbs or gel filters. Certain blue or ultra-violet shades can create a restful atmosphere.

Even with national advertising campaigns, low-energy lighting hasn't really caught on as much as the government and the environmentalists would have liked. Those tubular fluorescent bulbs that use only a fraction of the energy of a standard bulb do give off a dull yellowy light that just isn't sexy. I particularly dislike the way they flicker uncertainly into existence like an old television set when you switch them on. But if you care more about the planet or your electricity bill than the effect, tubular fluorescent lights are for you. They will last so much longer, and an 11-watt bulb will give off the equivalent light of a 60-watt standard bulb. Perhaps one day they will perfect low energy mains-voltage light that is crisp and white and comes on instantly.

Bathrooms and shower rooms of course need special light fittings that are designed and categorised for this purpose. Essentially they are housed so that the bulbs or lamps can be changed with one hand and sealed against moisture if they are located above a shower or bath. Since you need an extractor fan in a bathroom to remove the moist air (even if you have a window), those fans that are integral with a halogen spot lamp are ideal for locating above showers and baths.

The fan motor itself is built in-line to the ducting and not mounted on the ceiling as usual. This means it doesn't sit there looking like an oversized smoke alarm, and you don't get to listen to the fan whirring away whilst you bathe. In-line fans located within the ducting like this may also be sited between the floor joists of a floor above, again affording some valued sound insulation. On the ceiling all you see is the recessed halogen lamp sitting in the centre of a duct that is flush to the ceiling finish, making them aesthetically pleasing, functional, quieter and stylish. I wish I'd invented them myself.

A final comment on artificial light ought probably to be that we have far too much of it. Try reducing the amount of illumination in your homes; apart from reducing your electricity bill, who knows, your eyesight might thank you for it, and your children may grow up less afraid of the dark.

Finishings

As I mentioned before, perhaps the best finish for tanked walls is plasterboard secured on dabs of specialised adhesive, since there are no fixings to puncture the tanking and any out-of-plumb walls can be straightened.

If you are planning on hanging anything heavy to the walls, then ordinary plasterboard isn't ideal. What you really need is fibre-reinforced plasterboard. It doesn't sound like much, but these boards are reinforced with paper fibres compressed to a high density, making them a lot tougher. They need a handsaw to be cut. The manufacturers claim that you can hang 30 kg from a screw fixing in these wall boards or 17 kg from a picture hook. You can't do this with ordinary plasterboard and get away with it, not even with expansion fixings that open up behind the board.

Before the ceilings can be lined with plasterboard, the condition of the timber joists should be checked. If there hasn't been much ventilation down here in the past, as is more often than not the case, then the joists may have suffered from dry rot and need replacing, but otherwise a thorough treatment of preservative will be sufficient.

Heating

Depending on the proposed use of your basement, you may choose not to heat it or just to heat it to a low level. It's worth considering that if you are insulating the walls and floor to a high standard of thermal resistance, not much heating will be necessary for some uses.

A utility room or kitchen is likely to generate sufficient heat from its washing and cooking appliances. A boiler located down here will likely produce enough heat to maintain an acceptable room temperature.

If you do want to heat the basement – and central heating will definitely help to keep the atmosphere dry – then you might consider an underfloor heating system. These systems are becoming popular these days, and are easily added onto the existing central heating system, controlled by a roomstat that will treat the basement as a separate zone from the remainder of the house.

Underfloor heating was popular in the 1960s with the widespread system building approach to flats and new houses. Then it was electrical heating, but the recent revival is for water pipes of thin and continuous plastic tubing that are clipped to the floor insulation before the screed is laid encasing them, and through which hot water is pumped and circulated. The advantages are obvious:–

● You don't require wall radiators, which, to be honest, have never looked pretty, even when buried inside MDF latticework covers.

● You get to have ceramic floor tiles or even stone slabs that would normally be cold to touch, but here they will be warmed and comfortable to walk on, barefoot if you like.

● The whole room is heated to a constant warmth, instead of hot areas near the radiator and cooler areas away from them.

● The warmth will rise up uniformly, warming the house above as well.

This type of heating has been widely used in Scandinavia and Northern Europe, and has been very popular with people self-building their own homes. Because the pipework has to be fixed over insulation, some insulation manufacturers have been catching on for some time and are producing their boards with the channels already profiled in to accept the pipes, push-fit style. This has the advantage of a guaranteed pipe centre and reduces the labour time considerably. Once the pipes are in position, each end is connected up to a manifold.

It does make it difficult to install pipework to a suspended timber floating floor because of the labyrinth of pipes which must go over insulation to avoid inadvertently heating the ground instead of the room. Yes, the pipes could be notched into the joists, or the joists battened over to raise the floorboards, but this is horribly labour-intensive. Far better to secure the pipework to the insulation with the special clips provided and screed the whole lot in.

I did mention that it all has to be pressure-tested first, didn't I? Before the floor finish is laid, the pipes are placed under test to check for leaks. Once the floor screed is gone off you can always float a laminate floor, or boarding for that matter, over it if you crave a timber finish, but be aware that the boards may cup as they are heated and dried.

I can't think of a better way of heating a basement than underfloor heating, particularly if it's an odd-shaped area that wanders off round corners a bit.

If you still like radiators stuck on the wall and surface plumbing, radiators are available in a few different styles these days. The standard pressed-steel convector type – powder-coated and not requiring decoration unless you really want to remain effective; the old-fashioned cast-iron type you might find in a demolition site sell-off or architectural salvage yard is back in vogue with the Victorian look; or the ultra-slim wall panels that reach from floor to ceiling and are almost as thin as a mural for the modernist and minimalist among you.

The final choice is yours – just remember to install thermostatic controls whatever you use, so that the temperature can be automatically regulated as a separate zone.

Decorating

You could be forgiven for thinking that basements, devoid of much or all natural light, can only be decorated in white or pastel shades. And for the moment I'll agree with you.

121

Basement walls can look good in white, particularly if they contain kitchens. White says clean, it says hygienic, and above all it says bright. But it does need decorating afterwards – a splash of red or blue here and there, a picture of violent colour saturation hanging from the wall beneath a bright picture light, because without any colour at all white by itself also says institution and possibly whispers sanatorium.

Black might seem an odd choice for a basement, but it is an option – and not just for those 'specialist-interest basement' firms that custom-make wall shackles and leather tables. I am told that a black floor, ceiling and walls, together with a black tablecloth and chairs, are considered to induce conversation at dinner parties – probably along the lines of 'Has anyone brought a torch?', but on the other hand your guests might die of depression before the dessert arrives. Personally, I think an entertainment room, and I don't mean adult entertainment or sorcery, would benefit from a deep colour. Royal blue absorbs the light spectacularly without being gloomy, and recessed alcoves picked out in sunflower yellow lit by halogen spotlights look very effective.

Pastel shades aren't fashionable now at the beginning of the twenty-first century, but given a decade or two and they'll be right back. Assuming you couldn't care less about fashion, pastel shades will still reflect the light around down here whilst adding a touch of warmth and softness to the room. Bold colours are still fashionable thanks to an army of TV home-makeover shows, but you have to find one that you can live with, and finding the exact colour that at the same time creates an atmosphere for the room and is tolerable may not be all that easy.

Colour – the 'coup de grâce'

The opportunity in a room like this to do this something different with the decor is more prevalent here than anywhere else, perhaps using colour in a way that you wouldn't consider in the rest of the house. On the other hand, as a nation, we are said to be a bit on the colour-phobic (or chromo-phobic) side. Sincerity and importance are expressed by tones like burgundy and white for us, and if we want to trade up from seriousness to stylishness we tend to exchange burgundy and white for burgundy and cream. Vivid colour on our homes, as in our cars and office walls, says we are not taking things entirely seriously or, worse, that we are less than sophisticated and therefore culturally starved.

All this is a shame when you consider that the human eye can detect around ten million shades of colour. Actually, given our shyness with colour and the relatively limited choice available from the spectrum, it does explain why you can never find the exact paint you want on the shelf of the local DIY store.

My advice is to decide on the colour range from the primary choices and then add white until you've got the shade and tone that you can live with. You might be surprised at how a subtle lightening of a loud colour like yellow or red can make all the difference; or using magnolia instead of white will take some of the luminescence out of it and warm it a little. You can afford to experiment here, armed with a bucket full of match pots and some white paper plates.

Once you've got the exact colour you want, leave it stuck to the wall for a few days to see how it looks under different lighting conditions, particularly if you have some natural light down here, and then visit one of the many colour-matching paint shops that can scan any colour and analyse it by computer and then mix the paint in the quantity you need to that analysis. At least doing it this way will mean the paint is thoroughly mixed and pure, and if you need more than one tin, of course you can guarantee a perfect match, rather than the old-fashioned, rather hit-and-miss methods.

But even if you already have seen the colour you want and have a piece of it in your pocket, these paint shops will be able to scan it and make the paint. I am continually impressed by this. My granddad's profession was a colour mixer back in the beginning of the twentieth century – he mixed paint by hand – and, like my dad, I have an interest in paint and painting.

The reason you may be disappointed with the end result of your colour mixing venture can only be due to one of two things, or possibly both of them. One – the colour and texture of the wall you have applied the paint to, and two – the light you first witnessed the colour in. It may not be the same light it will enjoy in the room, and that can change with the seasons and the time of day. I have a dining room yellow with a hint of orange that positively glows with warmth in the early-morning sunshine but is cool in the afternoon. It isn't just natural light either; make sure your artificial lights are connected to appreciate how the colour works under different lamps. Remember that if you saw the colour on a terracotta tile basking in Tuscan sunshine it will not look the same in a basement room in Basingstoke, even if you brought it home to be scanned.

CHAPTER 6

Garages

The side life

It seems to many that the garage stuck on the side of the house could be converted in a moment to a usable room. And for some of us it could – but before we build this castle too high in the air, there are some things you should know.

Since the genesis of the modern housing estate in the 1960s, we have been building integral garages in our new homes. In our car-dependent world, off-road parking has become more and more essential, and to this day all but basic starter homes are built with a garage attached – which makes it all the more remarkable to realise that these garages are too small to be used for most of us to actually park and keep our cars in.

Cars come in all sizes of course, but integral garages in Britain do not. Usually they are 2.4 m wide and 5.5 m deep – the car park space standard dimensions. Of course in the UK we've become gradually accustomed to parking our cars in tight spots and having to squeeze out of them with the door only half-open, but having to do this in your own home is not so easy to accept. Imagine building the kitchen so that your family had to enter and leave, one at a time, with the door only partially open. You wouldn't do it, and yet developers build in the integral garage as if we all drive small cars. When was the last time you wandered around a show home and found a nice saloon parked in the garage? Invariably they've turned the garage into the office, which seems to work so much better.

In the USA, where integral garages are also standard in new home construction, the space is cavernous by comparison. In spite of having bigger cars with bigger doors, you can not only open the doors wide but, and here's the truly astounding thing, walk around the car with your shopping without the slightest worry of damaging the paintwork or yourself on the walls.

In Britain we continue to buy (and hence demand) garages with our new homes, and yet we know that if we can get the car in them, we might not be able to get out of it without using the sunroof – which is why so many of them are used to keep the lawnmower in and then converted into habitable rooms every year. With the up-and-over door replaced by a picture window and the floors and walls finished, garages make excellent rooms.

Planning consent

There are some drawbacks, however, and they start with the possibility of planning consent. We live in a congested corner of the world, many of our roads are choked with traffic, and not all of it is moving. In the evenings and at weekends there are roads in Britain's residential streets that are lined with cars on both sides seamlessly. Highway safety is compromised, people find it difficult to cross the road between parked cars, and emergency vehicles like fire engines are often prevented from using what remains of the narrowed street. Because of this, development that puts more cars out on to the roads is sometimes considered to be unacceptable development.

If your home is relatively modern, in order for it to have got planning permission and be built, a degree of parking space would have to have been provided, either by the garage or the driveway or both. Taking it or some of it away may be a problem. Planning departments usually have published design guides to work to and policies that stipulate the extent of parking a new home should have. Often they relate to the number of bedrooms the home has, the more bedrooms the more car space needed to go with it, the theory being that a three- or four-bedroom house may be occupied by a two- or possibly a three-car family.

But do you need to apply for planning consent in the first place? Possibly not.

The answer to that question revolves around the same issue – the date when the house was constructed, whether parking conditions were imposed on its original permission, and so on. The only to way to be sure if these apply is to write to your local planning authority with some details of your proposal and enquire whether a planning application is required. Even if it is, you may still have sufficient space outside the house to meet all your off-road parking obligations and gain approval without any problems.

Space to park

Of course you are going to want space for your car somewhere. But what you consider to be space enough may not be the same as what the planning office considers. Generally they are looking for that 5.5 m x 2.4 m box I spoke of earlier, but in addition to that they do like to see cars pulling out onto the roads in a forward gear. Reversing out onto a main road is often frowned upon, and so turning space might also be needed. Some bizarre arrangements have resulted from these requirements where space did not exist, sometimes involving turntables that spin the car around 180°.

Remember that it is space that matters here. For example, the parking space outside may be part of your garden; if you wish to park on the grass, then that is your business. In converting your garage, for example, you may have to rely on space in your garden to compensate, but the Planning Authority may still require you to have dropped-kerb access over the pathway. They may not be able to require you to extend the driveway or hard surface it, so long as the space exists – it is generally considered up to you as to how it exists, i.e. as grass, tarmac or gravel. The exception to this would be in the case of listed buildings, conservation areas and National Parks, etc., where extended planning requirements apply to preserve the character and appearance of buildings and localities.

Obviously if there are physical barriers such as garden walls, fences or street furniture in the way, then that isn't going to be considered accessible parking space, and Planning Officers do visit sites to consider planning applications. So remember that if you need to create some additional parking space to compensate for your garage conversion, this is worth bearing in mind. The Planning Officers will need to ensure that you have proper safe and access to it.

If that access means crossing another person's land or driveway, for example, some evidence of your legal right of way will be required. Invariably the owner's comments to your planning application will be sought anyway, so make sure there is no dispute over it and discuss it with them first. A verbal right of way may not be good enough, since they may sell up or change their mind at any time, leaving you cut off from your own parking space.

Visibility is important as well – being able to see down the road before you pull out on to it. Typically hedges, walls and other obstructions need to be low enough to be able to see over them, or splayed back. The minimum distance up the road you should be able to see is dependent upon the class of road.

Daylight

With the garage doors gone, you are left with a sizeable structural opening just crying out for a window. A window of toughened safety glass divided into manageable panes could be installed to the entire opening, although the heat loss from it could be extreme unless it was of the highest performing double-glazing. The standards for double-glazing have improved over the years, but of course as they do, so the minimum standards of the Building

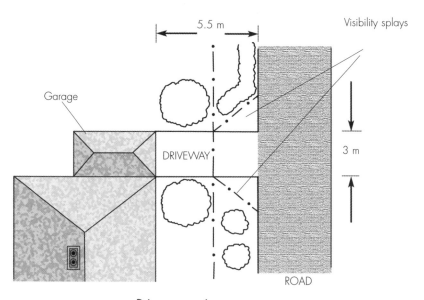

Driveway requirements.

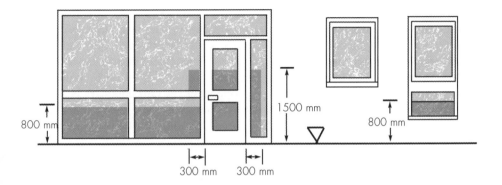

Toughened or laminated safety glass zones (shown darker).

ALLOWABLE AREAS WITHOUT FIRE-RESISTANCE NEAR BOUNDARIES

Closest distance to boundary from the wall	Maximum area of no fire resistance windows or doors	Wood or plastic cladding (no windows or doors)
less than 1 m	1 m sq	–
1 m	5.6 m sq	11.2 m sq
2 m	12 m sq	24 m sq
3 m	18 m sq	36 m sq
4 m	24 m sq	48 m sq
5 m	30 m sq	60 m sq
6 m or more	no limit	no limit

NOTES: *This table can only be used for homes up to 24 m in length. All areas of no fire resistance should be added together and the total area applied to the table.*

Regulations improve with them to keep pace, as they did in April 2002. This makes it much harder to outperform the Building Regulation requirements and justify having bigger glazing areas than would normal be allowed. A fully glazed garage door opening would make up at least 5 sq m of glass in a room where the floor area is no more than 15 sq m. It's likely that this amount of heat loss from one room will be a problem, unless you can compensate for it by having better than normal insulation elsewhere, particularly in the roof and walls.

From a design point of view, I like the idea of filling the whole opening with glazing, but it could prove expensive. A double-glazed unit comprising a 20-mm cavity filled with argon gas combined with glass coated with a low-emissivity film will achieve good thermal insulation, in fact as good as a solid brick wall. A window that fits the width but sits up under the existing lintel with a wall beneath it, is invariably the most common option. This does, however, mean you need to construct a weatherproof and insulated external wall beneath it.

Adding new windows to the side wall of a garage is another way of increasing the amount of light, and if you are proposing to divide the space up into two or more rooms, this could be essential. There is a possible problem if the side wall of the garage is close to or indeed on the boundary of your property. A boundary that is 1 m or less from the wall restricts the allowable size of a window to 1 m sq, but that is still sufficient to light a small

room. This restriction relates to the risk from fire spreading to other buildings.

If the boundary is with a public road or a railway, for example, where development can't take place, your 'relevant boundary' is actually the centre of that road, railway, etc. You don't have to own a share in it; this notional or relevant boundary is hypothetical because the risk of a fire spreading from your house to another is greatly reduced by the fact that nobody can build there to care about it.

These issues don't exist if you put the window in the roof and not a side wall. Choose to provide a skylight window in the roof, and you get so much more daylight anyway. These windows are available for flat roofs as

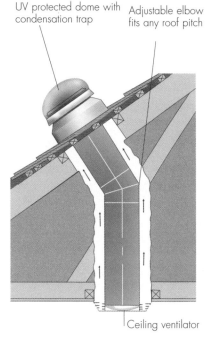

UV protected dome with condensation trap

Adjustable elbow fits any roof pitch

Ceiling ventilator

Solar pipe.

well as pitched although they tend to be glazed with polycarbonate rather than glass in the former. You might only have seen them on a larger scale in commercial buildings but they are available for all uses.

The last option for introducing daylight is the solar pipe that reflects the light down a polished tube installed through the roof. In a standard flat roof the pipe will only to be 125–200 mm long, and hence the daylight reduction will be almost nonexistent. These pipes were designed for situations like this, and if you have a longer garage where the back will be short of light, one would be ideal.

Walls

Given only a single-skin brick garage, some upgrading is required for both weather and thermal resistance. If you are not too bothered about losing some of the room width, then the best way to upgrade the walls is to build up a new blockwork skin or timber-frame skin on the inside behind a cavity. The two choices are different, both in insulation and weather resistance, so I'll deal with them separately.

Blockwork inner skin

Aerated or insulating blocks are obviously favourite, and you can buy them from 100 mm to 215 mm thick. They are extremely lightweight and can be built off the floor slab of the garage. Although they may need to be tied in at the top of the wall, with restraint straps for example, I would keep this wall independent of the outer leaf of brickwork. If the brickwork has piers

at no more than 3 m apart it will remain fine by itself without you needing to strengthen it with a cavity wall construction.

If the brickwork has suffered damage from strong winds (perhaps because it isn't supported with piers or buttressing walls at 3-m intervals), then you should look at strengthening the wall. In this case, using remedial wall ties to bond in the new inner leaf of blockwork would be an option. These remedial wall ties are available in two types: mechanical and chemical. The mechanical ones are inserted into a pre-drilled hole and tightened up much the same as anchor bolts are. The chemical sort are glued into pre-drilled holes by resin bonding.

One potential problem with creating a structural cavity wall like this is that you really want the whole thing built up off of the same foundation. Yes, that could mean breaking up the concrete floor slab at the edges and digging down to the existing foundation below ground level. If it is wide enough, you may be able to get the inner leaf built up off it without the need to widen it. If not, more work is required to get the concrete foundation widened to accept the new thicker wall. Therefore it is best to leave the existing brickwork as an independent wall from a structural point of view, unless it is showing signs of cracking.

The blockwork skin should be built up with insulation in the cavity, even if it is an insulating block. Building Regulations will require you to insulate to a minimum standard, but you should look for the most thermally efficient

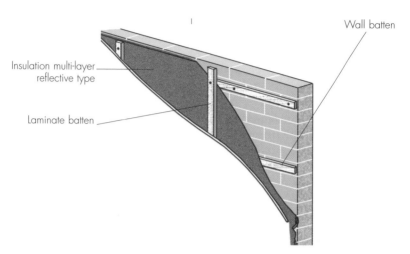

Reflective multi-laminate insulation between battens.

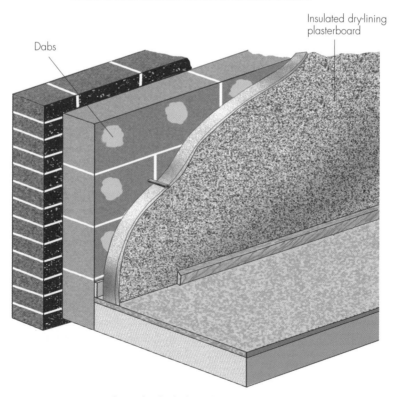

Insulation-backed plasterboard on dabs.

construction you can afford. Choices of insulating material range from mineral-fibre wool that comes in semi-rigid slab form, polyurethane boards that are totally rigid, and reflective multi-laminates of aluminium foil and foam that are totally flexible, thin and need supporting to the wall.

The first two types are traditional and have been around for the least ten years or more. They may be environmentally friendly in their manufacture (zero ozone depletion rated), but they are not so friendly to your hands when installing them. The fibres at the exposed ends are irritants and can become airborne. You should wear a suitable mask when cutting the sheets, and gloves when handling them, even for a short time.

The polyurethane boards are foil-backed in some cases, and have razor-sharp as well as airborne fibres when cut up. The reflective multi-laminate type materials are the best insulants by far, but they do need taping together at the joints. As they are reinforced with nylon mesh to make them untearable, they can be difficult to cut – only a new blade in your craft knife or the sharpest scissors will do it.

Whichever insulant you choose, you will end up with a warm cavity wall, but if you've built it up from the slab it will have needed a remedial cavity tray DPC built in at the bottom. Even as part of a cavity wall single leafs of brickwork are not very weather-resistant – rain borne on the wind can soak right through. The wall insulation will resist it, but rain will run down its outer face and need to be caught by a tray at the base

that channels it back to the outside via weepholes cut into the brickwork. If you came up off the foundation with the new skin for the structural cavity wall, then you should have a new DPC bedded at floor level to marry in with the floor's damp-proofing. In other words, the same as the normal way to build a cavity wall from scratch.

Timber inner skin

A timber-frame inner leaf would do just the same, but your carpenters will need to make up the wall in panels on the ground before they fix it in position. This is because the outer face of the timber framework will be covered by a moisture-resistant sheeting, tacked or even stapled to it. There is specialized material for this job that is vapour-permeable or 'breathable'.

You've probably heard that word 'breathable' a lot; even paint can be breathable these days. It comes from the fact that our homes can be moisture-laden with water vapour, not just from bathing and cooking but from us sweating and breathing out all day – a huge amount of water vapour is created, and if we don't have vapour-permeable walls that let it out, it will inevitably condense and start to cause damp problems.

So, fitting vapour permeable sheets here can keep the wall breathable. The reason the stuff has to go on the outside face of the timber frame and not the more convenient inside face is because the insulation will go between the frame studs, and it is on the cold, outer face of that where the vapour condenses into water.

10 Expert Points

HERE ARE TEN EXPERT POINTS TO
CONSTRUCTING ANY TIMBER STUD
PARTITION:

1 SIZE OF TIMBER
Timber studs should be no less than
38 mm wide and 63 mm thick. Normally
50 x 100 mm timber is used, but this can be
reduced as far as 38 x 63 mm if you are
tight for space, and where they do not
exceed 2.4 m high.

2 TOLERANCE
The studs should be no more than
10 mm out of level horizontally over
5 m, and no more than 10 mm out of
plumb vertically.

3 HEAD AND SOLE PLATES
The head and sole plates should be in
one length of timber and fixed at no more
than 600-mm centres.

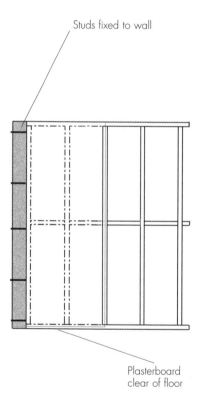

Studs fixed to wall

Plasterboard
clear of floor

Studwork partition.

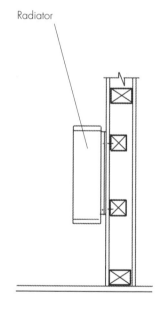

Radiator

Radiator fixing to studwork partition.

4 NOGGINS
Noggins should be tight-fitting between the studs and fixed at mid-height. In addition, all plasterboard edges should be supported by noggins.

5 PLASTERBOARD JOINTS
Avoid horizontal joints in plasterboard; fix full size boards upright, but make sure they don't touch the floor.

6 ABUTMENTS
Studs abutting to adjacent walls should be fixed at maximum 600 mm centres.

7 NAILING
All timbers should be fixed together using two no. 75 x 2.65 mm diameter nails.

8 SPACING OF STUDS
For board widths of 900 mm either 9.5 mm or 12.5 mm thickness, studs should be fixed at maximum 450 mm spacing. For board widths of 1200 mm, 9.5 mm thickness, studs should be at maximum 400 mm spacings. For 12.5 mm thickness, studs should be a maximum 600 mm spacing.

9 SIZE OF NAILS FOR FIXING BOARDS
30 mm for 9.5 mm plasterboard; 40 mm for 12.5 mm plasterboard; 50 mm for 19 mm plasterboard

10 FIXTURES AND FITTINGS
Extra noggins should be built in to support heavy fixtures like radiators, cupboards etc.

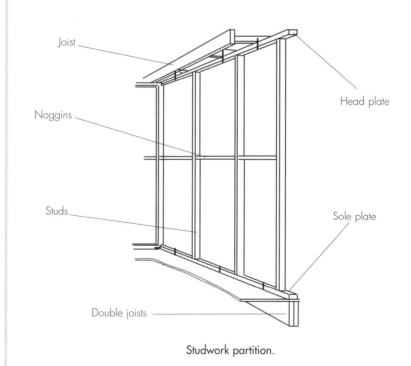

Joist

Head plate

Noggins

Studs

Sole plate

Double joists

Studwork partition.

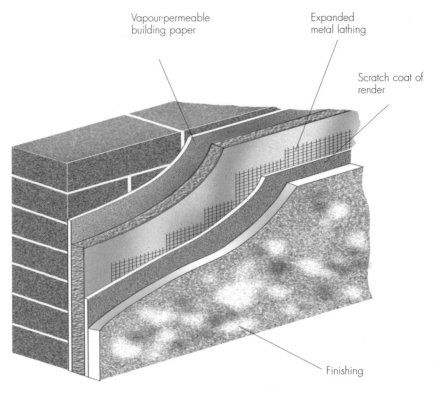

Vapour-permeable
building paper

Expanded
metal lathing

Scratch coat of
render

Finishing

External insulation and render.

Once the insulation is installed to
the frame, and for this job glass-fibre or
mineral wool 100 mm thick is ideal, the
wall can be covered with polythene and
plasterboarded over. Timber-framed walls
are superb for this job. The work is non-
skilled and can be done by DIY
carpentry if you follow some basic rules.

Exterior insulation

The biggest issue with garage
conversions is the width of the room.
As we've already established, the

standard British integral garage is not
exactly cavernous. With an extra inner
leaf wall built and finishings applied,
the width can be down to 2.2 m,
making for quite a narrow room. There
is one possible solution, and that is to
insulate and weatherproof the wall on
the outside. This is quite popular in
continental Europe and it is beginning
to see its way into refurbishment
projects here. Obviously there are some
provisos, not least of all a generously
overhanging roof to weather the top

edge, and if you have three external walls to treat this way, an offset garage where you don't have to maintain a building line is helpful. Given these factors, external insulated cladding could be the best way to deal with single skin garage walls.

Using rigid insulation sheets anchored to the outside of the wall with purpose-made remedial ties, the boards can be rendered over to form a warm and weather-resistant wall. Perhaps the best insulant for this is phenolic or polyurethane foam boards, which may only need to be 50 mm thick to achieve a 'U' value of around 0.4. If you can't add another 20 mm of render thickness with a traditional cement and sand render, you could opt for a two-coat lightweight polymer modified render used in a thinner application.

If you don't want to render at all, you might be able to board the wall with shiplap or weatherboarding, in which case the insulation boards could be pinned between horizontal timber battens before being covered by a 'breather paper', vertical battens and finally the boarding. It is important that the breather paper and counter-battening go on so that a ventilated cavity exists behind the boards.

Depending on how close you are to the boundary of your property, timber-boarding the outside may not be possible since it presents an external fire risk to some extent. The same solution with vertical hanging tiles made of clay or concrete will not.

You should check with your local planning authority before embarking on any of these external cladding options, since they all change the outer appearance of the garage.

Weather resistance

Much of the remaining work in these projects is geared towards making sure your converted garage is weather-resistant. The roof coverings, for example, will need to be checked for leaks and if necessary overhauled or replaced. Old bitumen felt flat roofs may be suffering from cracking and blistering and need replacing.

The floor slab may not have been laid over a polythene damp-proof membrane, and the concrete could be damp. Sealing it with a paint-on damp-proofing liquid will prevent the damp from getting through to the finishings.

The driveway outside may need chopping back away from the garage door opening if it was raised up to meet the garage floor. It should be kept back at least 200 mm and the gap filled with drainage shingle if the level isn't at least 150 mm below the damp-proof course.

Finally, the abutment of the garage roof to the house may well need a cavity tray damp-proof course. If the wall is a brick outer skin cavity wall, a cavity tray will stop rainwater from penetrating it and running down the cavity to reappear in your converted room below – an occurrence that may not have mattered greatly for a garage, but will for a habitable room.

Vents, fascias and soffits

One of the side effects of insulating the roof of your garage conversion is the risk of creating condensation in the roof void. Only by adding a cross-flow of fresh air to the cold space left above the insulation can you be sure of preventing vapour from condensing there and breeding damp and mould.

If you have a wide soffit to the garage roof at present, then the easiest solution is to install some remedial vents to it. The plastic circular ones are favourite for this job since they require no disruption to the roof finishes. All you need is a hole cutter of the right diameter and a device for twisting them in, both of which of course far exceed the cost of the vents themselves. The hole cutters work fine in wood or plywood soffits but find cement-fibre soffits hard going.

If you aren't blessed with a wide soffit (and not everybody is), you shouldn't be tempted to install these circular vents in the fascia; wind-driven rain will penetrate unless you can be sure that guttering will totally protect them. Instead, you may have to replace the existing boards with new and built-in ventilation. PVC-U is the popular choice since it removes the need for any future maintenance, and in the past re-painting fascias has always meant having to remove and replace the guttering.

Some builders will cover the existing boards with a thin PVC-U over-cladding, but I can't help thinking that this will not last for long as the wood sweats and rots beneath it. Much better to go for a thicker board that will fix direct to the rafter feet once the old boarding is removed. Look for one with a ventilated soffit pre-slotted to provide the air flow.

Although the fascias and bargeboards may be around 16 mm thick, soffit

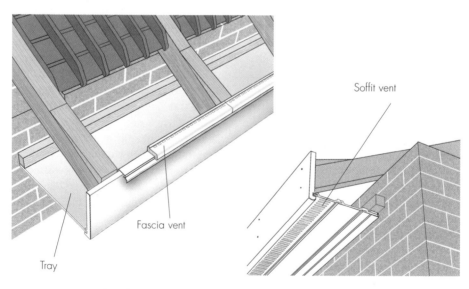

Fascia vent

Tray

Soffit vent

Fascia vent and insulation retaining tray.

PVC-U fascia and vent soffit.

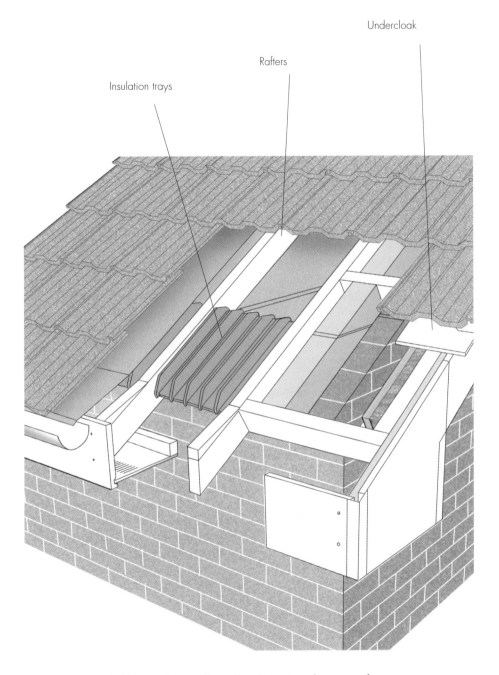

Undercloak

Rafters

Insulation trays

PVC-U ventilated soffit and insulation trays between rafters.

boards are often only half that, and hence these should not be wider than about 200 mm. A very wide soffit is going to need some extra support or thicker material.

Roof ventilation

It is essential to install vents at the eaves and ridge positions to allow air in and out. A common mistake is to pack glass-fibre insulation in between the rafters without leaving space for an airflow over the insulation. This will cause condensation to build up within the construction. It is important to check that a gap of at least 50 mm is retained for airflow on the cold (outside) face of the insulation.

If your rafters are only 100 mm deep, you are faced with the choice of either making them deeper to accommodate the necessary thickness of glass fibre, or using a high-performance insulation board such as polyurethane foam, which can achieve the same in a much reduced thickness. The first option is easily achieved by nailing timber battens to the underside of the rafters.

Exterior cladding

If you don't like the look of PVC-U cladding and are unable to choose timber boarding so near to the boundary, then you might consider one of the cement fibre-based alternatives available. They tend to come with a long-term guarantee of up to 50 years, and are available in timber-like grain finishes, either pre-coloured or left to be decorated to your choice. This could be done with gloss, external acrylic-based emulsion or even a water-based wood stain. The material does look a bit too perfect to pass off completely as natural wood, and I'd resist the urge to try and do that, but in white it's as good as the PVC-U stuff and it comes with fire resistance that you can't get from plastic or wood.

Timber boarding

Timber is coming back into fashion. We are in an age where raw and natural materials are not only appealing to us visually but help to remind us of our place in the natural world. Wood is the most environmentally friendly material available to us in building – it contains no nasty toxins, it is renewable, breathable, biodegradable, doesn't deplete the ozone layer and generally looks nice. A real all-rounder.

Some countries, notably those with rainforests, still continue to plunder their natural resources without renewal, and for this reason alone timber should be sourced to make sure that it has been forested from a managed and sustainable environment. Labels such as the FSC (Forest Stewardship Council) symbol are displayed on timber products derived from stewarded forests, those where trees are harvested and replanted in a managed cycle.

Europe's tree population is said to be better now than it was a hundred years ago, with more being planted than felled every year. Unfortunately, this is not the case in some parts of the world, where logging continues to deplete ancient forests at a frightening rate. With customers becoming aware of the need to buy only timber from sustainable origins and avoiding the rest, the forests of the world stand a better chance of being preserved and managed for the future.

Maintaining timber in good decorative order is where we've always had our problems; wood stains don't last forever, gloss paint peels off and the timber itself remains flexible, swelling and shrinking with the changing seasons. Leaving timber to a more natural finish and free from protective coatings may be the answer – in doing so, we are freeing ourselves of the maintenance tasks for life that we hate so much, as well as enjoying the natural appearance of timber.

Some species are ideal for this, Western red cedar in particular. Cedar has been used for many years, both in this country and North America. It has a different cellular structure to other woods that reduces its combustibility, making it ideal for buildings; it looks and smells great and it has excellent weather-resistance. On the downside it does age to a silvery grey patina which looks nothing like its original appearance. In order for cedar shingles to keep their original attributes they have to be periodically well oiled – a process which slows down, rather than prevents ageing.

Services

Electrics and electricians

The garage is often the home of the electrical distribution board, and there is no need to re-site it now that it has become a room. You do need, however, to make sure that it is safe, particularly

that there aren't any blanks or covers missing from the fuses or MCBs. The board can be enclosed within a cupboard if you would rather hide it, or if you feel it needs updating anyway (it might be one of the old-fashioned re-wireable fuse boards), you could have your electrician replace it with a new MCB board and a casing that can be decorated with the room.

Having the distribution board here makes it ideal for installing a new circuit for the garage room alone, although a sub-circuit can easily be installed for one extra room.

Either way, you should seek to obtain from your electrician a Certificate of Installation. The trade associations produce their own standard forms, but your electrician is at liberty to produce his or her own certificates. It is a legal requirement for a tradesmen carrying out works on electrics to provide a certificate; the only person exempt from this is you, as the home-owner working on your own property.

For alterations to existing circuits you can expect to receive a Minor Works Certificate under BS:7671, and for new circuits, a Standard Electrical Installation Certificate under the same code of practice. Both certificates relate to the installing and the testing of the work.

Here's the thing about electrical work in England and Wales: anyone can do it. Just the same as anyone can operate as a builder, anyone can operate as an electrician. After all, the materials are freely available from DIY shops along with free advice on how

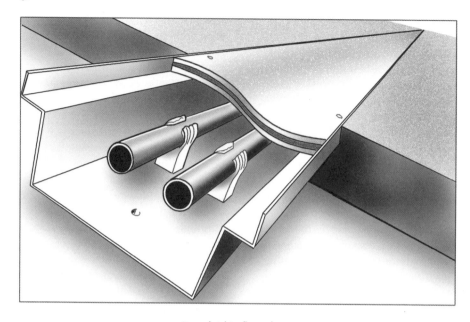

Pipes laid in floor duct.

to use them. And the other important thing about electrics is you can make it work without it being necessarily safe. The controls, if you can call them that, that are applied are in the form of guidance documents.

The IEE (Institute of Electrical Engineers) Wiring Regulations are, in spite of their statutory-sounding title, not able to produce legally enforceable legislation or standards at all. Perhaps one day they will be included in the Building Regulations (England and Wales) and only registered electricians following them will be able to trade, but then, on the other hand, given the track record so far, maybe not.

Wiring regulations are all about safety, and extend to such things as wrapping a black common wire in a light switch with red duct tape to indicate that it is the switch live, a warning to anyone working on the switch in the future. At the other end of the safety scale, they cover extra precautions for bonding in special areas like bathrooms, where the risk of electrocution from being wet and naked is increased.

Electricity has been with us in our homes for over a hundred years now and it hasn't changed in all that time; what has changed is how much we use it. Our demand for more and more power grows continuously, and the need to ensure that our circuits and sockets are able to safely deliver it is essential.

It makes sense to use only qualified electricians who are registered with the ECA (Electrical Contractors Association) or the NIC (National Inspection Council), both of whom offer free warranties with their members' work. These warranties cover the installation for a number of years against any defects or non-conforming work (non-conforming with the IEE wiring regulations applicable at the time of installation). A claim against these warranties will result in the work being inspected by the Association and verified before remedial work is carried out to bring it up to scratch.

A large number of electricians are registered with the ECA or NIC, perhaps most of them, but they don't have to be, so don't assume that yours is. Check it out first. Members have to have their accounts audited for three years trading before joining, and their financial probity and business acumen are examined as part of the process of registration.

Their insurance-backed warranties also provide you with cover against the electrician going bankrupt before they finish the work. At the insurer's cost, the work will be completed by another registered firm. Ask your electrician for the full details of these warranties.

Plumbing

If you have more than just the electricity supply coming into the house via the garage – gas or water, for example – you might want to think about providing a walk-in service cupboard or utility room to house them. Boilers are ideally located in utility rooms. If they are gas-fired, only a CORGI-registered plumber can install them or work on them. This is about the only mandatory registration scheme we have. Gas has obviously killed more people than electricity over the years, and CORGI-registered plumbers and heating engineers have to maintain their training every three years to stay registered – at great expense to themselves. Their work doesn't come cheap as a result.

If you have supply pipes on the surface, you may be able to box them in and hide them from view during the conversion work. Plastic ducting can be installed around existing pipes once the pipe clips are removed, to enclose them, or you could have your carpenter make up some MDF accessible pipe ducts to fit.

Since the Water Regulations of 1999, all new jointed water pipes have to be accessible and laid in ducts through the floors or walls, so they can't be completely be buried in the structure. It's a nuisance during the installation achieving this, but I guess you'll be grateful if you ever have a leaking joint and need to get at it. The ducts can be bought purpose-made or formed on site by your builder.

CHAPTER 7

Barns and Outbuildings

The outside life

Rural homes and older town homes are often blessed with outbuildings that have fallen into redundancy. Whether they be large barns or small coal sheds, they have great potential to be converted and brought back into use. The extent of the work involved in achieving this varies tremendously from one building to another, and is dependent on several factors, its original construction, present condition and the use you propose for it among them. In this chapter, I have sought to advise on some of the more universal elements of such conversions.

Strengthening timber buildings

Racking resistance is the act of stiffening timber structures by bracing several members together, reinforcing the whole element. The individual studs of the walls could all shift out of square if the wall was not braced for racking resistance. In old timber-framed buildings, traditional racking was done with diagonal braces cut between the studs, although the boarding on the outside also contributes to racking resistance. In many modern barn conversions, plywood or OSB sheeting is fixed over the outside of the frames before the boarding is replaced to achieve this in lieu of diagonal bracing.

This latter is the common and most efficient and economic solution if you are insulating and plastering between the posts to cover it up from the inside. The sheets are best nailed with improved nailing like annular-ring shank nails that are of high withdrawal resistance – once hammered in, they ain't coming out. The result is that the wall panels act as a solid and rigid wall, rather than a series of individual posts.

Roofs can also suffer from racking in old barns, although in modern construction and conversion, battening out the roof with timber roofing battens to fix the tiles to does the job quite efficiently.

If you are fortunate enough to have a traditional barn alongside your home, you may wish to convert it as an annexe for a dependent relative or simply as occasional accommodation for yourself or guests. If you work from home, you might prefer to convert it to a studio or for workshop use. The latter are sometimes more favoured by planning authorities over residential conversions, because they tend to reflect the rural importance of old barns, and the work can be done with more sensitivity to the building's architecture.

The traditional barn might be timber-framed, or a brick- or stone-walled building with a thatched, slate or tile roof. The wonderful thing about barns is that their very design reflects their location. Unlike the buildings we construct today, that look identical whether they are in Kent or Yorkshire, barn builders made use of local materials exclusively and built them to a regional style.

Since the Norman Conquest, barns have been used to store crops and straw from harvesting, but they became

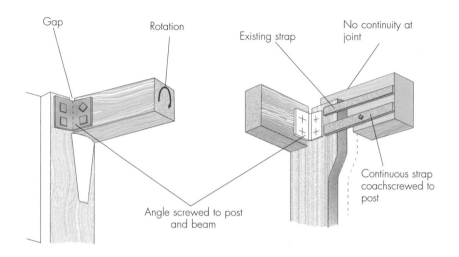

Gap

Rotation

Existing strap

No continuity at joint

Angle screwed to post and beam

Continuous strap coachscrewed to post

Fitting a continuous strap.

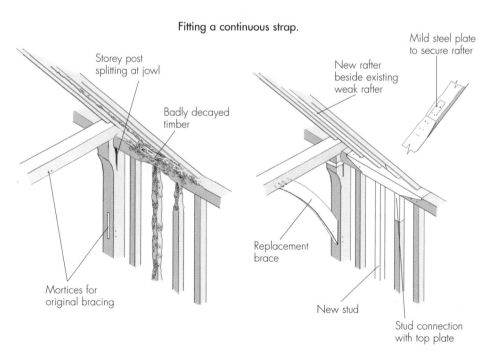

Storey post splitting at jowl

Badly decayed timber

New rafter beside existing weak rafter

Mild steel plate to secure rafter

Replacement brace

Mortices for original bracing

New stud

Stud connection with top plate

Fitting new timber braces and replacing studs.

Stair and gallery
free-standing
structure rather than
wrapped around
side wall

Fully glazed door
opening

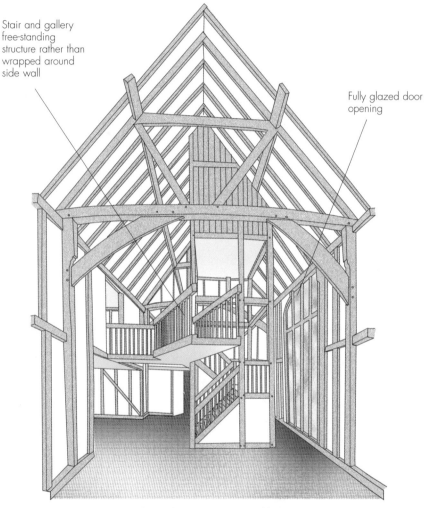

Interior of a 20th-century converted barn.

redundant with modern farming methods. If your barn is of historical or agricultural significance, or if it is located in a conservation area or special landscape area, for example, the conversion will have to retain the true character of the building and engage structural repair as opposed to putting up a replacement.

I think that in spite of the stringent rules imposed on converting old barns back into useable buildings, the idea is

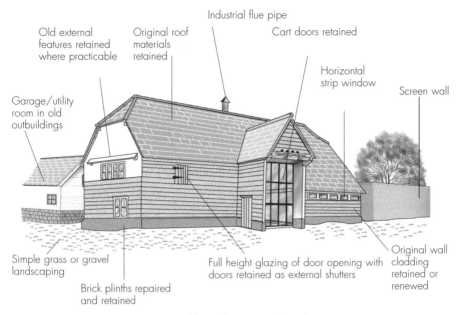

Old external features retained where practicable

Original roof materials retained

Industrial flue pipe

Cart doors retained

Horizontal strip window

Screen wall

Garage/utility room in old outbuildings

Simple grass or gravel landscaping

Brick plinths repaired and retained

Full height glazing of door opening with doors retained as external shutters

Original wall cladding retained or renewed

Typical barn showing public side.

a noble one. Buildings that aren't used are on a time limit towards collapse and oblivion. Only through conversion and use do we save our barns, so don't be mistaken for thinking the word 'preservation' means 'leave alone'.

Traditional barns usually consist of individual bays inked by aisles, often with a central projection like a porch, called a midstrey, that was used for storing the hay wagons overnight, hence the large cart doors on the front of the midstrey. The big cart doors also let in plenty of daylight and ventilation during the working day for the workers threshing crops on the barn floor. Barn floors were normally made of well-compacted soil like chalk to produce a hard surface for this purpose. It is often a good advantage in a barn conversion where solid concrete floors are introduced, to know that the sub-base

to the floor is sound. Those big doors usually face the prevailing winds in the area to provide maximum circulation for drying the corn. From here the grain was removed and stored in a granary. Your barn may have smaller doors at higher level; these are drying doors to promote air circulation. Often a catslide roof extends down to 2 m or less above the ground on one side or at one end.

The 1980s saw more barns, granaries and oast houses converted into executive homes than ever before or ever since. My own borough had the highest number of conversions in the country. For the most part, they were all done the same. The cart doors were removed and a purpose-made glazed screen replaced it, with an entrance door fixed in the opening. Behind that sat the largest entrance hall anyone

could want, complete with a staircase running up to a first-floor gallery. The upper floor itself was usually divided into small bedrooms with en-suites here and there, and rooflights. The ground-floor designs tended to be open-plan largely, with rooms divided only by dwarf brick walls and open studwork frames. As much of the oak frame was exposed as possible and beeswaxed to a finish.

These conversions were very popular

and probably still are, and of course at the time everybody thought they were as good as they could possibly be. Opinion has changed a bit since then. Current thinking tends towards retaining the barn appearance with the cart doors left on, the minimum amount of small windows installed, and conservation-style rooflights. Current thinking also tends toward not turning them into executive homes. The advice on barn conversions covered in this

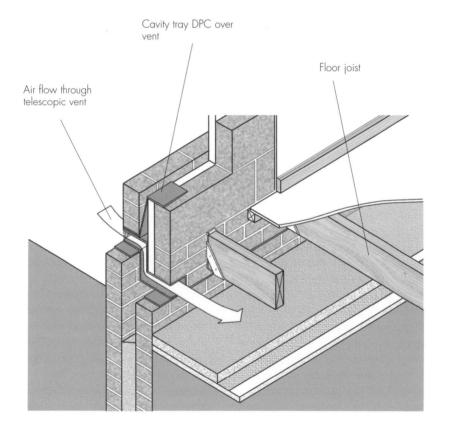

Underfloor ventilation by air bricks.

Air flow straight
through air brick

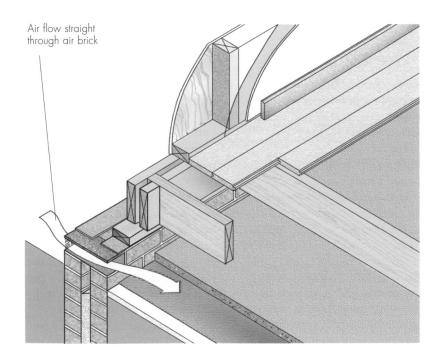

Suspended timber floor with air-brick vents.

chapter is not aimed at creating new dwellings but at making ancillary use of them, adding to your home.

Foundations

The first problem with converting an old outbuilding into habitable use begins beneath the ground. If it was built long ago or if it was an agricultural building, then it is quite possible that it wasn't constructed from much of a footing. That won't be a problem if it isn't suffering from subsidence at the moment and if the conversion simply reinstates the building without increasing its weight. But if you are adding a floor, loading the roof with some nice tiles where only sheeting was before, or constructing new walls, then the foundations should be called into question before you do anything else.

Only by exposing foundations with a few trial holes can their adequacy be assessed. The shape, size, depth and condition of the foundations should be determined. These exposure holes should be dug carefully by hand to avoid undermining the foundations or damaging them. You also need to know what the ground conditions are like, how strong the subsoil is, whether it is water-laden or desiccated, and whether it is affected by nearby trees.

Trees close to outbuildings

If the building hasn't been used for much over the years beyond storage, then the presence of trees quietly growing nearby may have been ignored.

I have seen trees growing out of the roofs of old barns and sometimes out of the walls. Usually they are ash or sycamore trees, which have an amazing propensity for reproducing themselves in odd places. With their gyrocopter seed pods, they are superb colonists and can grow to a good size in a few short years. As nice a feature as they may make, young trees growing too close to the building have got to be rooted out. The best way to do this is to cut them to a stump, drill a hole in it for one of the proprietary (systemic) root killers to be injected, and wait.

Those that are close enough and big enough to be affecting clay soil by desiccation are another matter. If the tree is large and mature enough to be depriving the soil of moisture every summer, then removing it could lead to severe clay heave for years to come. If

you're undecided on whether to leave the tree and underpin the building, or whether to root it out (and perhaps still have to underpin the building), you should consult an arboroculturist. They should begin their work by establishing whether the tree is older than the building or vice versa. If the tree is the older of the two, then there is a risk in clay soil, that the heave caused by removing it could be worse than the subsidence by leaving it.

Underpinning

Underpinning the existing foundations means extending them deeper to find better strength or stability from the ground. Traditional underpinning means forming a new foundation beneath the existing ones in a series of short lengths, carried out to a predetermined sequence. British Standard 8004 gives advice on underpinning and how it should be carried out, and you may wish to refer to it in your specification to the builder.

Repairing old timber floors

Whilst it is unusual for barns and agricultural outbuildings to have timber suspended floors, other outbuildings may well have. Old timber floors are often rotten in neglected buildings, particularly around the edges if the joists are built into the walls. If only the joist ends are decayed, it could well be possible to cut off the affected bits and resupport them from metal joist hangars. The old joist holes can be filled with mortar, and you could well have saved yourself the cost of replacing the joists.

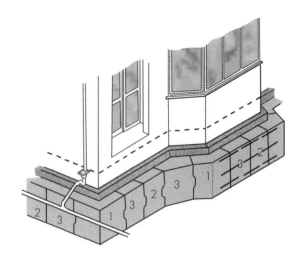

Underpinning sequence in numerical order.

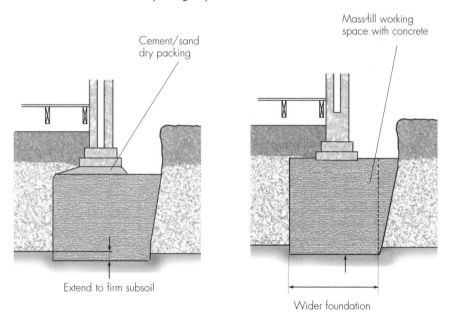

Cement/sand
dry packing

Mass-fill working
space with concrete

Extend to firm subsoil

Wider foundation

Mass-fill underpinning.

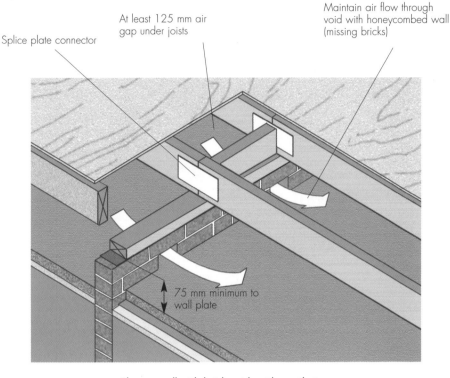

Splice plate connector

At least 125 mm air gap under joists

Maintain air flow through void with honeycombed wall (missing bricks)

75 mm minimum to wall plate

Sleeper wall with brick voids with ventilation.

If you're not that lucky, and the rot has spread further back on some of the joists, you could repair them with cripple joists. A cripple joist is a short length of joist that runs alongside the older one with its decayed section cut out, supporting it like a splint. The joist should overlap by at least four times the depth and be bolted together with at least four M12 bolts. Toothed plate connectors should be used with the bolts to prevent any movement. You really can't do this to all of them, or any of them if the joists are less than 150 mm deep, but it is a good way of repairing a few.

Timber ground floors can also have debris in the void beneath them. Take the opportunity to clear out any rubble or litter, which will only serve to promote fungal or insect attack in the future. When the rubble is cleared out, a gap of at least 100-125 mm depth should exist beneath the joists, sufficient to let air flow through. The ground should be at the same level as that outside.

Ventilation beneath a suspended timber floor is important; without it, dry rot is almost a certainty. Airbricks should be built in to the walls, if they aren't already, at just below the joist

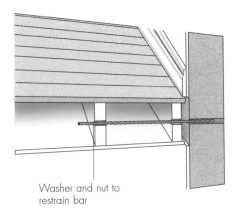

Washer and nut to
restrain bar

Tie bar to floor and wall.

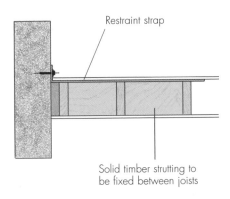

Restraint strap

Solid timber strutting to
be fixed between joists

Adding lateral restraint to floors.

level. Some might exist, but are there enough? You are looking for the equivalent of at least 1500 sq mm of air space per metre length of wall. Let's try that in English: those clay air bricks that are brick size let in enough air to mean they should be spaced at 1.5-m centres. The plastic ones are much better (more hole, less brick) and will normally go in at 4-m centres, but they are often considered unsuitable in appearance for use in valued older buildings.

If there are sleeper walls beneath the floor joists supporting them in the middle, they should be honeycombed to let the air through. The timber plates on the top should be bedded to a DPC.

Brick walls and damp-proofing

It should come as no surprise to you to discover that your brick outbuilding has no damp-proof course, or if it does

have one, it is deteriorated and the masonry is suffering from rising damp. Easy to resolve in brickwork, not so easy in flint or stone walls, but then these are less susceptible to rising damp in the first place.

In brick walls a damp-proof course of silicon can be injected into the brickwork to form an effective barrier against rising damp for many years to come. Often alongside timber treatment, DPC injection is a service covered by specialist contractors who may offer a 20-year guarantee. Sadly, alongside double-glazing the industry has developed a bit of a bad reputation for diagnosing rising damp at every opportunity when in fact damp is penetrating from a leaking roof, broken rainwater pipe or some other reason wholly unconnected with rising damp.

It is less of a problem when converting small brick barns or outbuildings, because the existing DPC is likely to be conspicuous by its absence, but that doesn't mean that the job can't be badly done – this is specialist work, and the injected DPC won't work if the fluid quantity isn't regulated or if it is injected at the wrong level or, most commonly, if it is injected into damaged brickwork. Since the walls have to be drilled with a series of holes into which the chemical is injected, the damage can arise from the drilling itself. The system only works if the DPC is continuous, and therefore broken and crumbling bricks will create gaps in it which could let damp through.

For this reason alone it is a good idea to check the masonry over before and after the pre-drilling has been done to see what sort of condition it is in. Areas of damaged brickwork are going to need replacing first. The manufacturers of chemical DPCs do specify how much fluid must be injected per metre of wall given its thickness, and the installers should keep a record of how much fluid they have used. This won't matter in outbuilding conversions, but the chemicals contain volatile solvents that give off odours for a few days after the work has been done.

It is important to realize that leaving residual damp in the walls will mean you cannot use a normal gypsum plaster inside as this can draw hygroscopic salts out of the wall. Instead, special renovating plaster should be used that is resistant to these salts and dampness. It should be applied for at least 1 m above the height of the DPC.

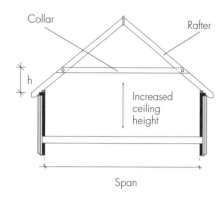

Raised collar roof.

Roofs

By far the most popular form of roof construction for any outbuilding conversion is the open roof or raised tie construction. By raising the ceiling height to higher ties, you are opening up the building to more light and air. Increased headroom is created, if not on the ground floor then on a first floor, that may not have been possible without converting the roof this way.

Structurally, there are complications, however. The roof can spread and push out on the walls if the ties are raised too high. The table on page 153 and diagram above give an indication of what is structurally possible when altering the original roof.

The table on page 153 assumes:

● that the rafters are bolted to the ties with M12 bolts and double-sided toothed plate connectors

RAFTER SIZE	TIE OR COLLAR SIZE	H (MAX)	SPAN BETWEEN WALLS
38 x 150 mm	38 x 150 mm	325 mm	up to 5 m
38 x 175 mm	38 x 175 mm	450 mm	up to 5 m
50 x 175 mm	50 x 175 mm	575 mm	up to 5 m
50 x 150 mm	38 x 200 mm	325 mm	up to 6 m
50 x 175 mm	38 x 175 mm	525 mm	up to 6 m
50 x 200 mm	38 x 175 mm	725 mm	up to 6 m

- that the roof pitch is between 30 and 55 degrees

- that the timber is C24 grade (SC3 or GS)

- that the rafters and ties are at 400 mm spacings

- that the walls are cavity brick/block construction

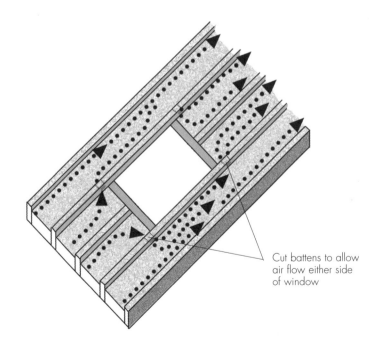

Cut battens to allow air flow either side of window

Roof ventilation around a rooflight.

153

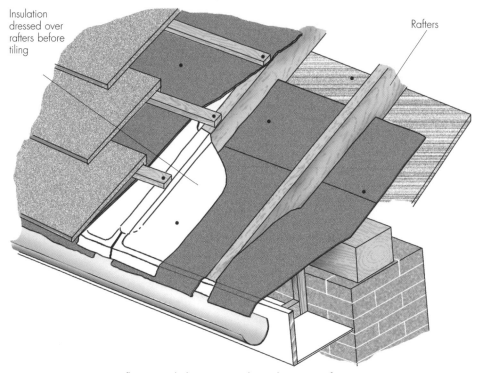

Insulation dressed over rafters before tiling

Rafters

Reflective multi-laminate insulation between rafters.

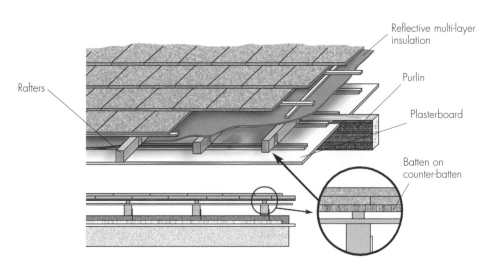

Reflective multi-layer insulation

Rafters

Purlin

Plasterboard

Batten on counter-batten

Multi-layer insulation over rafters can increase headroom.

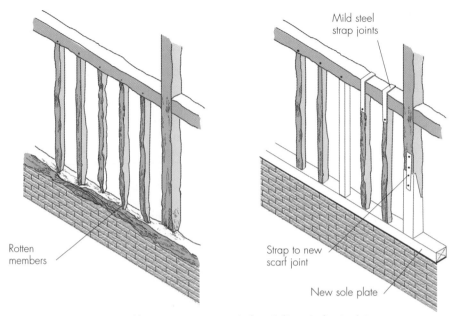

Post and beam joint repairs – before (left) and after (right).

Treating fungal and insect attack

Insect attack

Most buildings in their lifetime will come under attack from wood-boring insects, and the chances of finding insect damage in an outbuilding are quite high, since they may have been left to do their boring in peace for many years.

In the UK the most common wood-boring beetle is the furniture beetle. In spite of its name, it is quite happy to attack structural timber as well as furniture. When inspecting for insect attack, specialists look for the presence of dust, known as frass, left on the wood from boring, and for fresh flight-emergence holes.

Most insecticide is contact-based and so the beetles don't actually need to eat it to die, but simply to come into contact with it. It is sprayed or brushed onto timber, which not only contaminates the newly hatched bugs as they emerge but also prevents them from laying more eggs in the treated wood.

One method of keeping furniture beetles at bay is to thermally insulate the outer envelope of your barn so that the timbers themselves are kept within the heated space. Furniture beetles need a moisture content to the timber of at least 12 per cent, and by bringing all the wood inside to the heated fabric of the building, the timber will be kept drier than this. In practice this means creating a warm roof with the insulation overlaying the rafters before the tiling is replaced, and insulating over the outside of the stud walls, for example, before the cladding is secured. Both are common design choices in converting timber-framed barns, and are easily achieved.

Fungal decay

Decaying timber must be cut out and burnt off-site, but that doesn't mean the new wood or what remains of the old should be ignored. It must be treated with preservative to prevent the outbreak recurring. The treatment of existing timber against rot or insect attack is fundamental to all conversion work, and there is no shortage of specialist companies offering variations of this service.

Look for a company that is registered with the British Wood Preserving and Damp Proofing Association. Companies should carry out their work in accordance with the Association's Code of Practice, and if they don't you will have somebody to tell about it.

Usually they will survey the building, report on its problems and identify the nature of rot first. Before it can be treated efficiently, you have to know the true cause. In the UK, our timber is at threat from furniture beetle, powder post beetle, deathwatch and, in some areas, longhorn beetle. Occasionally termites on holiday – introduced by accident – are found, but as yet global warming isn't enough to encourage them to seek asylum here.

Timber fungus is either wet or dry rot, two very different species requiring different treatments. Look for the brown darkening of the timber common to both types. Oddly enough, wet rot can sometime bleach the timber, making it lighter – something that dry rot never does. Dry rot can also cause wood to crack across the grain, and as if that wasn't enough of a repertoire, dry rot can attack brick walls as well.

What has caused the fungal attack is important. It might have simply been the old leaking roof, the broken downpipe or the absence of a damp-proof course, all of which your conversion work will be correcting – but what if it was something else? The exposed wall that is hit by a prevailing westerly wind, driving the rain through, will still be there when you've finished the conversion. If it is a problem, only cladding the wall outside with timber boarding, tile hanging or rendering will cure it. The same applies to groundwater problems that may need to be alleviated by land drainage.

The survey findings should have identified or at least suggested the cause of problems, but, as is often the case with conversions, it is only when you start to open the building up that you begin to appreciate the full extent of its troubles.

Your warranty for the success of dry-rot treatment won't be worth much unless it is possible to remove the cause of the damp. In these situations you might be offered a 'limited' warranty that describes the treatment as palliative. Avoid accepting these if you can – they are basically saying they'll do their best to reduce the fungal infestation but can't guarantee to eradicate it.

Because wet rot will not spread to good dry timber but remain only where it has a high moisture content, it isn't always necessary to treat the good timbers that haven't been affected.

1:2:9	cement : lime : sand (should be protected against frost for at least seven days)
1:1:6	cement : lime : sand (as above)
1:6	cement : sand (standard mix)
1:4	cement : sand (a strong mix – plasticiser additive should be used)

Repointing brickwork

In renovating an old brick building, the very least you can expect to do is repoint the brick walls. Repointing is the mind-numbingly boring act of raking out the old mortar joints between the bricks and refilling them with fresh mortar. If you are the sort of person who finds weeding the garden therapeutic, then you might want to do this job yourself rather than employ somebody. For this reason alone, I've included some extra detail for DIY use.

Because you only want to do the sections of masonry where the mortar is crumbling or actually missing, the trick is to ensure that the mortar mix is correct and will match the existing mortar when it is fully dry. In some situations the mortar on an entire wall will have eroded back from decades of weather exposure. The wall could be significantly weakened and its weather resistance compromised by this, so repointing it is not just a cosmetic makeover.

● The old joints need to be raked out to a depth at least twice the thickness of the joint and not more than 35 mm. Normally this would mean somewhere between 15 mm and 25 mm deep.

● If you are raking to a depth greater than 25 mm, this should be done in small areas at a time, no more than

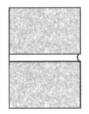 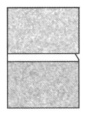  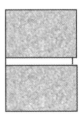

Mortar joints, from left to right: bucket handle; weather struck; flush; recessed.

three courses high and three bricks (1 m) long. This will avoid potentially weakening the wall during the process.

● The joints should be washed down to remove dust and loose mortar before they are repointed.

● You should resist the urge to make the new mortar mix harder with a higher proportion of cement, as this can lead to the bricks themselves spalling or the mortar cracking when it shrinks. Instead, aim to match the colour of the existing mortar by trying several mixes on a sample area, if it looks a bit white, it may contain lime in the mix. Traditionally lime was used instead of cement, and then later with cement to produce a more flexible mortar that was essential with flintwork. Some examples of mortar mixes are given in the table on page 157.

● Make sure that only enough mortar for two hours work is mixed at any one time.

The choice of pointing finish varies tremendously, but you may be forced to duplicate what exists already if you are working in areas only.

If, on the other hand, you are doing a complete wall or building, the finish you use should be chosen by both appearance and the degree of exposure to the elements. A 'bucket handle' finish (more easily done with a round stick than an actual bucket handle) is

best for weathering, and so is 'weather-struck', which directs the rainwater out.

The least weather-resistant of all is a full recessed joint that exposes the edges of the bricks or a flush struck joint that isn't recessed at all. Some examples of the pointing finishes mentioned here are shown in the diagrams on page 157.

Repairing woodwork

Not many of us go to the trouble of repairing old wooden windows any more. If they are that bad it is probably better to replace them, but if they are valued or only partially rotten, then arresting the decay and repairing them may be appropriate.

Before the 1970s timber windows were not pre-treated with preservative, and as a result, the decay of windows older than this has been inevitable. Usually the cills and frame edges in contact with the masonry are affected first. Where the joints in the frame have shrunk back and water has got in or where the glazing putty has fallen out, decay is bound to follow.

Before you can decide whether it is more economical to replace the window than repair it, you need to establish the extent of the decay. Pressing the blade of a pocket-knife into the wood will determine how far the decay has got, so probe around the frame gently. If the rot is purely on the surface, it could be possible to scrape it away and treat the remaining wood with preservative. This can be applied by brush in three coats, with each coat allowed to fully soak in before the next is applied, or it could be pressure-

applied by a specialist installer. Once
the solvent has evaporated, the wood
can be repaired with an epoxy-resin
wood filler and sanded to its original
flush finish ready for decoration.

Repairing broken timber beams is a
bit more of a specialist venture, but
given the cost of replacing a significant
oak beam, for example, one that is
quite important.

Rendering old brick walls

With climate change bringing us
warmer but wetter weather, solid
brickwork may not be enough to
ensure a weathertight outbuilding.
Instead, you may need to introduce
some cladding, if not to all the outside
walls, then to at least the most
exposed elevation.

Rendering is one of the most
effective forms of cladding, but if it
isn't done correctly it will be
guaranteed to fail in a few short years.
Here are the three most popular ways
of making a bad job of it:

● **Poor preparation of brickwork**
The wall should be cleaned off,
with raked out mortar joints to
form a key, and if necessary a
bonding agent should be applied. If
you are intending to use an
expanded metal lathing to bond to,
three coats of render should be
applied rather than two.

● **Incorrect mix**
The mix of cement and sand should
relate to the strength of the wall
behind; too strong a mix would
cause the render to crack and spall

off. The same will occur if the base
coat is stronger than the top coat.

● **Inappropriate weather conditions**
The weather for rendering has to
be just right: not too hot so that it
doesn't go off too quickly, and
certainly not wet or raining – and
most certainly never when there is
a risk of frost. If a frost attacks
render before it is fully cured, it
will destroy it to the point where it
will need hacking off and doing
again. For this reason alone,
rendering tends not to be done
during the winter months.

Asbestos removal

Plenty of older buildings still contain
asbestos. Barns and redundant
outbuildings are frequently covered by
asbestos corrugated sheeting, which
was the cheapest way of keeping the
weather out. These roofing sheets are
the most commonly seen of all asbestos
cement products, but in addition to
them, gutters, rainwater pipes and
water storage tanks were also made
from the same material.

Indeed, it is surprising to know that
asbestos cement in this form was used
up until as recently as 1999. Other
types of asbestos used in building,
notably blue and brown asbestos, were
prohibited earlier, in 1985. This material
was once commonly used in spray on
coatings, pipe lagging and insulation
boards. The lagging and the insulation
are likely to be the worst to deal with
since they are very fibrous and contain
up to 85% asbestos. In the case of
asbestos cement, the asbestos content

is reduced to between 10 and 15%, but more importantly, it is bound and compacted into the product and is only therefore harmful when it is broken. Smashing up corrugated asbestos cement sheeting to dispose of it is a common threat, for in the process of doing so fibres can be released and become airborne.

Why are asbestos fibres such a threat? Because inhaling them can lead to diseases of the lungs and chest, like asbestosis or even cancer. The more fibres that are breathed in, the higher the risk of disease. Some 3000 deaths occur annually in Britain as a result of asbestos-related diseases. Until the dust or fibres are released the material is safe, but if you are engaging in conversion work on a building where it is present, any sawing, cutting or drilling into the material will achieve this.

Identifying and removing asbestos from buildings has consequently become specialist work, and you should seek a suitably qualified contractor for the purposes. Look for a company that is accredited by UKAS (the UK Accreditation Service) and licensed by the HSE. It will need to work in accordance with the Health and Safety Executive's guidelines and have liability insurance cover for this type of work and training certification. Evidence of these should be requested.

It isn't always necessary to remove the material – sometimes it can be sealed in, or enclosed to render it safe. The latter is only a good idea if you can guarantee that it won't be disturbed in the future or damaged. If you go down this route, you should mark your building plans to show exactly where the asbestos is, and make a note as to how you have contained it.

If you do need to remove it, your licensed contractor should carefully bag it up into double-layer polythene sacks, label it and taken it to a licensed waste disposal site that accepts it – normal household waste sites do not normally have a facility for dealing with asbestos. Your local authority or nearest HSE office will know where the closest site to you is.

As the building owner, you have a duty of care to tell your builders about the presence of asbestos in the building – and not just builders, any workmen installing facilities or services that may disturb it by fixings or whatever. They will need to wear protective clothing, a respirator, and to keep the material wet. Under no circumstances should you let them break up large pieces to make them easier to handle or remove, or use dust-creating power tools on it. Protective clothing should be disposed of rather than washed afterwards. If in any doubt, contact the Health and Safety Executive yourself for advice or your local authority's own Health and Safety Officer.

Drainage

If you intend to provide a WC, bathroom or kitchen to your outbuilding and connect the drainage into the existing system supplying your home, you will need to ensure that the depth of the existing drains is sufficient to make the connection.

Using PVC-U shallow access drainage means that you can, if necessary, resort to very shallow falls or gradients of the drains and still find they work. 1:80 is the very shallowest of gradients recommended by PVC-U drainage manufacturers, and laying pipes to gradients like this needs a lot of care. To the eye, it won't be possible to see whether it's level, or even falling backwards, come to that. A 1.2-m spirit level is essential to check the fall exists and that it's going the right way.

Cut plastic pipes need to be cut square and the ends chamfered to slide easily into the joint collar. Only purpose-made lubricant should be used to ease the joint together. For a standard 100 mm diameter pipe, 10 mm granular bedding or pea shingle should be used to sit the pipes on and surround and cover them before backfilling the trench with soil. Sometimes the sealing ring in the joint can become displaced or soiled by grit during the work, and this will cause the joint to leak. For this reason it is essential to place the pipework under a water test or air test before the trench is backfilled.

With a plug sealing the lowest end of the pipe, the system is filled with water from the highest manhole and left for several hours to monitor any change in the water level. There may be a little evaporation in hot weather, but otherwise the water level needs to remain constant. Any drop is likely to be a joint failure somewhere. In an air test, special u-tube gauges called manometers are used with a plug at both ends of the pipe to measure its airtightness. Before the system is tested, a strip of plastic poked in the

joints may tell you whether the sealing rings are correctly located in each.

Sometimes plastic pipes (which now come in up to 6-m lengths) arrive bent on site, and laying them in a straight line or to a straight fall can be difficult. You might find that filling them with water for a day or two will straighten them out from the weight of the water.

Electrical services

Electrical cables come in all different sizes for different currents. This is because there is inherent resistance in the cable to the flow of electricity, and resistance creates heat. Too much heat can cause electrical fires or risk of burning, which is why cables have to be rated and large enough to ensure they don't overheat, and why you can't encase them within the insulation of your roof space or wall.

The fuseboard on modern homes (1985 onwards) usually has MCBs fitted instead of fuses. These miniature circuit breakers are tiny electro-mechanical switches that do the same job as fuses and limit the size of the current passing through the circuit. If you overload the circuit with too many appliances, the MCB or fuse breaks the circuit. It goes without saying that you are not meant to keep on replacing them without finding out why this is happening. Because of these factors, extending your home's electrical supply to an outbuilding requires a calculation of how much wattage is to be used. You can do this quite easily with lights and other appliances because their power output is always printed somewhere on them or in the appliance manual.

10 Expert Points

TEN POINTS TO GUIDE YOU TOWARDS
A BETTER BARN CONVERSION ARE:

1 FACING MATERIALS
Look towards keeping the original
materials, whether they be bricks, roof tiles,
slates or timber boards. Seek to replace only
what is damaged and defective, and do not
be tempted to achieve the appearance of a
new building by replacing a whole roof
covering or wall with a new and
different material.

2 DETAILED SURVEY
Have a detailed survey of the barn
carried out before any other design work
is done. This will help you to understand
how the individual members relate to each
other. All of the structural elements can be
marked on a freehand-drawn plan – cross-
sections through the building are particularly
good for this.

3 CHARACTER
Aim to maintain the character of the
building both inside and out, by exposing
the principle structural elements inside and
trying to avoid renovation work that alters
the style and structural design of the building
under consideration.

4 INTERNAL PARTITIONS
Avoid too much dividing up of the barn
internally. Where partitions must be formed
to provide bedrooms and bathrooms and so
on, offset them from the principal frame
members to create a junction that can be
exposed and is structurally supportive.

5 WINDOWS
Look to include as small a set of
windows as you can, and locate them
between the studs of the frame. Large
picture windows are usually inappropriate in
converting agricultural buildings.

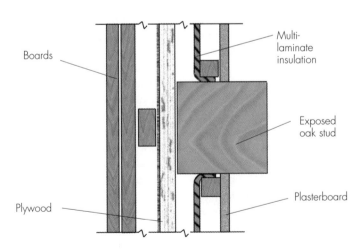

Insulating exposed timber stud walls.

ROOF WINDOWS
Avoid new dormer windows that alter the roofline. Instead, look for rooflights that are designed for use in conservation work. A lot of thought has gone into their design, so make use of it.

MULTI-USE CONVERSIONS
If you are planning on dividing up a large barn for separate uses, or individual units, try not to lose the unified appearance of the building externally. This may mean locating doors on different locations to avoid a terraced appearance.

CHIMNEYS
Chimneys do not normally exist in original barns, so the only alternative is the double-insulated rigid flue pipe that can

serve Agas, boilers and fireplaces alike. Alas, they tend to be polished stainless steel and emerge from the roof like an Apollo rocket, so take care choosing the position of appliances and style of flues.

REPAIRING TIMBERS
Rather than replacing whole members that are defective at just the ends, you should look towards cutting away the decayed timber and repairing them with traditional jointing methods, like splicing.

BROKEN TIMBER
Main beams and posts that are broken may be repairable with metal plates or chemical resin and reinforcing bars, so repairs can either be made into a feature or concealed.

RCDs (residual current devices) can be fitted to the fuseboard as an extra to the big on/off switch, so that if the current is unstabilised by bad insulation or damaged cables anywhere on the circuit, the power is instantaneously cut off. This will give your entire home – not just the conversion – a valuable safety feature.

The least your electrician should provide you with in connecting a supply to your outbuilding is an RCD on the radial circuit that runs outside. This can be done by a hard-wired unit inside your home, even if the supply is taken off of a spur.

Spurs are extensions of existing circuits, and if your electrical demands are moderate in the outbuilding, then a spurred connection may be sufficient.

Residual circuit breakers
RCDs come with little stickers explaining what they do and how to test them. This is because it is part of the Electrical Regulations that such a notice be displayed next to it. The notice is quite wordy and has be in letters at least 4.5 mm high, so if you do locate an RCD from a spurred connection within a room, you may wish to choose a position for it that discreetly hides it behind furniture (which can be easily be moved when you need to get at it). I've yet to see a TV makeover show that illustrates how displaying a electrical safety notice in the lounge can be brought in with the pseudo-Georgian décor.

The government, by the way, has gone sign mad, requiring builders to display signs about boilers, septic tanks, energy efficiency and everything – presumably not in an attempt to sabotage TV makeover shows but to elbow us into keeping house log books.

Outdoor cables must be run through special ducting to prevent them from accidental damage. Black polyethylene duct is used for electricity (yellow for gas and blue for water). Cables should be run outdoors in places where they are unlikely to be disturbed. In a cultivated garden they should be at least 500 mm deep, or 300 mm below paving if they are buried.

Your electrician will have to use at least 2.5 mm sq toughened cable and external weatherproof junction boxes if they are needed outside (to run feeds to garden pond pumps, for example), with the cable run through approved ducting. Without the ducting you can use armoured cable, but personally I feel most comfortable with cable that has been laid in ducting along the bottom of a wall or surface, and where I know its precise location.

Earth bonding

Earth wires are the most important component of an electrical installation. The earth is the safe escape route for electricity that has gone astray. If the wiring in your metal storage radiator, for example, was faulty, instead of charging the metal case of the radiator with electricity for you to come along and touch (with likely fatal consequences) the earth conductor would take most of it safely away. But here's the thing about earth bonding – it has to be continuous for it to work.

You can trace the earth bonding right through the house to the main protective conductor and the main earthing terminal. Below-ground supplies go back to the electricity supply company, which has an earth terminal. In rural areas with overhead electricity supply, copper rods buried in the ground can provide the main earthing point.

Power sockets

You can ask your electrician to provide any number of socket outlets on a ring circuit for you (and people often do), because it is unlikely that you will be using them all at the same time. Hence no limit is placed on the number. However, there is a limit on the area the circuit encloses (the room area) of 100 sq m (1075 sq ft) because the rulebook boys thought this was a better way of controlling the risk of overloading. Ring main circuits are normally run from a 30- or 32-amp fuseway in 2.5 sq mm cable. You can ask your electrician to run off a spurred cable to supply your outbuilding, but you are limited to how many power points you can have served by a spur, unless it is a fused spur which in itself will control how much you take off of it.

Your electrician may recommend that your outbuilding has its own distribution board so that a separate power and lighting circuit can be run out from switched MCBs. An RCD can be fitted as standard on this distribution board. If it is only a small outbuilding conversion with little in the way of power points and lighting, check with your electrician to see if this can be avoided and the lighting circuit can be extended out from the power circuit via a fused connection unit fitted with a 5-amp fuse. You can still have the RCD fitted at the point where the supply comes out of your home.

Heating

The easiest way to heat a small outbuilding is by electric radiators, which should be wired to fused connection units. Buy the units with neon lights that tell you when they're switched on if your radiator doesn't have an on light. Be warned that electric radiators have high-energy consumption, and this will have some bearing on the type of supply wiring you install to the building. Many radiators run at 3kW, the equivalent of thirty 100-watt light bulbs, making them uneconomical to use.

For larger buildings underfloor electric heat pads can be built in beneath floor screeding and controlled from a roomstat, providing a more efficient space-heating solution.

If you do choose an oil, gas or solid fuel heating system, spare some thought to the volume of the space you intend to heat, and not the area. With barns being converted to the roofline as open-galleried buildings, the heat can gather up there and never reach the centre of the room. Conventional radiators do a good job of letting the heat rise up the wall and sloping ceiling, rather than pushing it out. Underfloor heating, as described in Chapter Five, is also ideal for outbuildings where radiators may look out of place on exposed timber stud walls. An Aga, stove or fireplace placed centrally in the building will generate a lot of heat itself without the need for radiators at all, but specifying the appliance and the flue that it will need is not so easy and requires plenty of thought.

Solid-fuel stoves

Wood-burning appliances are a popular choice: the fuel is cheap, they are often small and architecturally designed, but they sometimes produce such little heat that they are more decorative than functional. Check to see what the rated output of the appliance is and relate this to the volume of air you are trying to heat with it.

One aspect of wood-burners is a problem: they give off a tar-like residue that in time can build up in certain flues or chimneys, creating a fire risk. Rigid insulated flue pipe systems without bends are suitable, but those with flexible liners or bendy flues can allow the residue to build up and shouldn't be used.

Any combustion appliance, whether its an open fire or a boiler, needs air for combustion and for ensuring that there is no spillage of fuel gases. How you bring that air to the appliance will depend on where it is positioned, what fuel it burns and just what type of appliance it is.

Kitchen ranges have become fashionable again, and if your conversion features kitchen space then a range may be just the thing for it. They can be fuelled by oil, gas, solid fuel (coal and wood) and now even electric. As electric appliances need no ventilation

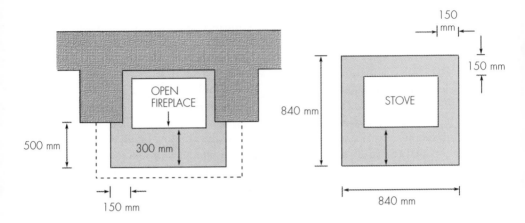

Minimum dimensions of hearth.

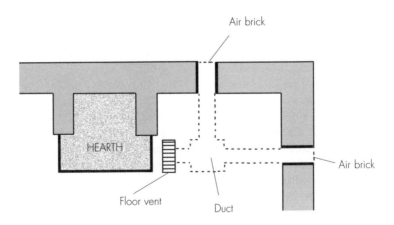

Combustion floor vent to fireplace.

for combustion, the latter have one less thing for you to worry about.

Stoves or open fires tend to be placed within fireplaces built against an outside wall. They make a feature of the wall, and the flue or chimney itself becomes a feature of the outside wall, but it is the worst place from which to heat the house – if you actually want to heat the place with it, then you need to place it as near to the middle of the building as possible. A central dividing wall could be used for this purpose, or the fire itself could be located within an isolated brick pier, as an island of warmth within an open space.

Modern stoves are factory-insulated and can be free-standing rather than built into brickwork. They can also be used to fuel hot water to a storage tank or even to supply radiators via a pumped system. New stoves now have thermostatically controlled boilers if hot water production is required as well.

A very rough guide to sizing a stove can be employed from the ratio obtained from a cubic foot to a cubic inch. The actual volume of the room in which the stove is located is calculated in cubic feet and the volume of the stove's fire chamber in cubic inches. Manufacturers usually specify the rated output in kW or BTUs (British thermal units) and the fire chamber size. To make sure you're on the right track, there are 3400 BTUs to 1kW, and that is enough heat to warm a room volume of about 12 cu m to 20° Centigrade when it's freezing outside.

If you are combining space heating with hot water production, you should add on 10,000 BTUs (approximately 3kW), and if you are supplying radiators with heat via pipework remember that as much as 20 per cent of the heat dissipates out through the pipes and not the radiator itself. One square foot of radiator employs around 200 BTUs (60 watts).

Wherever you position your stove or open fire, it has got to be built on a constructional hearth of non-combustible material, usually concrete, but potentially stone or brick. It has to be at least 125 mm thick, but consider that if you have a solid concrete floor you already have some of that thickness, and a non-combustible finish may be all that is needed.

One thing, though: the weight of a chimney and the appliance could be several tonnes, and a foundation may be required. The size of the hearth in area and how far it projects into and around the fire is also covered by the Building Regulations, with the aim of making sure that combusted fuel doesn't spill out and set alight to floor furnishings.

You also need a gap of at least 300 mm between floor and stove front if the stove can be operated with the door open. If it has to be sealed shut to work, then the distance can be reduced to 225 mm.

Coal burners

Coal burners produce soot in the chimney as opposed to the tar of wood burners, but it amounts to the same potential fire risk if the burner isn't maintained. Because coal produces a greater amount of heat than wood, a lot more fresh air for combustion is

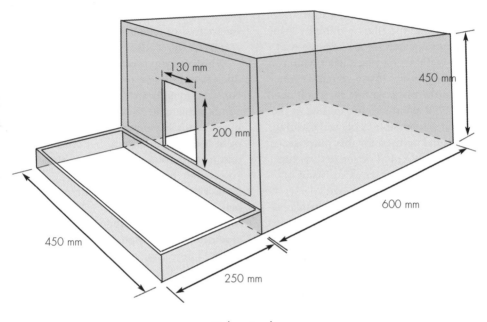

130 mm

450 mm

200 mm

450 mm

600 mm

250 mm

Owl nesting box.

required, and this is where the requirement can become a bit stringent in open fires.

An open inglenook fireplace with a massive throat opening will need a large vent or vents to keep it alight, but too big an opening and you won't be able to light the fire in the first place without holding a sheet across the top of it to help it draw.

Inglenook fireplaces look great, but efficient they are not. If you really do like the idea of a huge oak bressumer spanning between old brick jambs and all that, you can still have it with a

solid-fuel stove in the middle instead of an open fire basket. That way you get the look with the efficiency and cleanliness, and if you really must watch the flames dancing, you can always choose a stove that will operate with the doors open.

Environmental choices

Electricity is said to be the cleanest fuel because using it produces no air pollution – only the way we manufacture it does that. But given wind farms and solar energy, you could believe that in the future it could be our only truly green power. Wood creates a lot more smoke than modern coal fuels like anthracite, so although its harvest and supply may be green, actually burning it isn't. If you still would like to use old-fashioned house coal that produces smoke, you should buy a stove that has a smoke-eating second chamber built in a secondary burner, otherwise the smokeless coals are the norm.

Most stoves do not like to be left ticking over gently as background heaters; they are designed to be fired up and used at maximum capacity. Doing so helps keep the flue or chimney clear of soot and tar, and helps the fire gas rise quickly.

Wildlife homes

Barns and outbuildings may make ideal space for children or guests, but they also make ideal homes for other species. At the very least, locating a bird box high up on the gable end will create an instant starter home for some feathered lodgers.

With a little more effort you can accommodate barn owls by building an interior nest box into the conversion. Enclosing a small section of the roof void with external-grade plywood walls and providing a large enough entrance hole will be all that is needed for one of Britain's most endangered species to roost. The Hawk and Owl Trust will be pleased to send you details of their exact requirements.

An overhanging eave with open rafters not only keeps the weather off the walls (by providing a rain shadow) but also creates a building plot for house martins and swallows. Like barn owls, swallows have suffered a lot from the demise of agricultural barns, and designing in some space for these summer visitors would be much appreciated.

Swallows look for a bit of a ledge on which to build their mud nests, whereas house martins are quite happy to suspend one between wall and rafter. Yes, they can make a bit of a mess, but I felt a lot more sympathetic to their cause when I discovered that young swallows weren't just nipping around the corner when they left in September, but flying 10,000 km to South Africa before they were even five months old. If they breed successfully from your barns' eaves, they will return to it every summer.

Bats can also be housed within tall birdboxes that instead of holes have openings underneath, allowing them to just flap in and hang themselves up for the day. All of these species will reward you by keeping down the insect and rodent population in your garden, as well as giving you something to watch from the window *dolce far niente* – or even when you've got absolutely sweet nothing to do.

Enjoy your conversion!

Glossary

AAV
Air-admittance valve. An anti-vacuum valve that allows a regulated amount of air into a plumbing system but none out.

Aisle
Where the roof slopes down to the lower eaves level, the barn is extended parallel to it – this space is called the aisle.

Arcature
The style of architecture of an arch.

Ashlaring
The load-bearing timber stud wall that supports the roof.

Balanced flue
A room sealed flue that lets in the air supply and out the exhaust gases.

Bonding (plaster)
Lightweight plaster with vermiculite added to for two-coat plastering.

Bonding (electrical)
The earthing of metal pipes and fittings by connecting them to earth wiring to prevent electrical shock.

Casement
The hinged and opening part of a window.

Circuit breaker
A pop-out switch that acts as a fuse to prevent electrical overload.

Casement

Combi boilers
Combination boilers heat water on demand in pressure systems, without the need for storage tanks.

Consumer unit
Also called distribution board, a panel that holds MCBs or fuses for the home's electrical supply.

Crown post
A short post emerging off the centre of a tie-beam that rises up to the ridge.

DPC
A damp-proof course incorporated in walls to resist rising damp.

DPM
Damp-proof membrane built into a concrete floor. Usually polythene, but can be liquid bitumen.

Flashing
A sheet cut and fitted around joints in construction to weatherproof them.

Flitch beam
A site-formed beam comprising of two timbers with a steel plate between them, all bolted together.

Joist
Horizontal structural timber making up a floor or ceiling.

Jowl
The name given to the thickening at the top of the posts on medieval barns.

Knee
In a right-angled joint between a post and cross-beam in traditional building, the knee is the curved piece with the diagonal that braces the joint. Often cut from the tree at the joint of a branch and the trunk, a knee is a usually very strong. In 18th-century barns, knee-braces appear everywhere, but before then were used much less frequently.

Levelling compound
A floor finish material of latex that is self-levelling up to 6 mm thick.

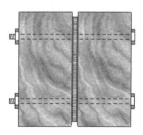

Flitch beam

Newel
The post at the top or bottom of a staircase fixing the handrail.

Noggin
A small piece of timber used between other main structural timbers to stiffen them.

PAR
Acronym for planed timber (prepared all round).

Pressure system
A sealed heating and hot-water system with a pressure valve instead of a vent in the header tank. See *Combi boilers*.

Pitch
The angle of the roof.

Purlin
The horizontal structural timber in a roof supporting the rafters often halfway up.

PVC-U
Polyvinyl chloride (commonly known as plastic).

Radial circuit
A type of electrical circuit like a ring circuit but fed from one end only.

Rafter
The sloping structural timbers of a roof supporting the tile battens.

Racking
The name given to the movement of an element due to wind loads.

Ring circuit
An electrical circuit for power sockets that runs around the home, joining up socket outlets, and then back to the distribution board.

RCD
Residual current device. An electrical contact breaker that monitors the earth wiring and switches the power off instantly if live current crosses to it.

Render
External or internal base coat plaster.

Riser
The uprights between the step (tread) of a stair.

Sarking
A roofing felt also used behind wall cladding to provide extra weather resistance.

Screed
The level floor finish of cement and sand, between 50 and 75 mm thick, applied to concrete floors.

Set
The finishing coat of plaster on a wall or ceiling.

Skim
The thin finishing coat of plaster applied over plasterboard.

Soffit
A decorative horizontal board used to cover the underside of overhanging rafters at the eaves.

String
The side board of a stair supporting the treads and balusters.

Sub-base
Also called hardcore. The substrata of fill material beneath a concrete floor.

Tanking
Waterproofing of walls and floors below ground level

Trussed rafter
A factory-manufactured roof member jointed with metal plates in a web of triangular shape. The members of each truss act holistically and not in isolation, so they cannot be cut or altered without damaging the truss.

TRV
Short for thermostatic radiator valve, fitted to radiators to switch off at a pre-set but adjustable temperature.

Wend beam
What we now call a collar, a high-level tie-beam between rafters that ties them together.

Winder
A turning tread in the stair.

Useful Contacts

Arboriculture Association
Ampfield House
Ampfield
Romsey
Hampshire
SO51 9PA
01794 368717
www.trees.org.uk

Association of Building
Engineers (ABE)
01604 404121
www.abe.org.uk

Association of Plumbing and
Heating Contractors
14–15 Ensign House
Ensign Business Centre
Westwood Way
Coventry
CV4 8JA
024 7647 0626
www.licensedplumber.co.uk

Bathroom Manufacturers
Association
Federation House
Station Road
Stoke-on-Trent
ST4 2RT
01782 747123
*www.bathroom-associa-
tion.org*

British Wood Preserving and
Damp-Proofing Association
Building No 6
Office Village
Romford Road
London
E15 4EA
020 8519 2588
www.bwpda.co.uk

Building Employers
Confederation
020 7580 5588

The Council for Registered
Gas Installers (CORGI)
1 Elmwood
Chineham Business Park
Crockford Lane
Basingstoke
Hampshire
RG24 8WG
01256 372300
www.corgi-gas.com

Electrical Contractors
Association
34 Palace Court
London
W2 4HY
020 7313 4800
www.eca.co.uk

Energy Savings Trust
0800 512012
www.est.org.uk

Environment Agency
0645 333111

Federation of Master
Builders
Register of members
www.findabuilder.co.uk

Glass and Glazing Federation
44-48 Borough High Street
London
SE1 1XB
020 7403 7177
www.ggf.org.uk

The Hawk and Owl Trust
www.hawkandowl.org

HETAS Ltd
PO Box 37
Bishops Cleeve
Gloucestershire
GL52 9TB
01242 673257
www.hetas.co.uk

The Institute of Plumbing
64 Station Lane
Hornchurch
Essex
RM12 6NB
01708 472791
www.plumbers.org.uk

Interior Decorators and
Designers Association Ltd
1-4 Chelsea Harbour Design
  Centre
Lots Road
London
SW10 0XE
020 7349 0800
www.idda.coluk

Institute of Structural
Engineers
020 7235 4535
www.istructe.org.uk

Kitchen Specialists
Association
12 Top Barn Business Centre
Holt Heath
Worcester
WR6 6NH
01905 621787
www.ksa.co.uk

National Association of
Scaffolding Contractors
(NASC)
020 7580 5404

National Fireplace Association
6th Floor McLaren Building
35 Dale End
Birmingham
B4 7LN
0121 200 1310
*www.nationalfireplaceasso-
ciation.org.uk*

National Inspection Council
for Electrical Installation
Contracting
37 Albert Embankment
London
SE1 7UJ
020 7564 2323
www.niceic.org.uk

Office of the Deputy Prime
Minister (ODPM)
Planning Inspectorate
0117 372 6372
Building Regulations
020 7944 5746
www.odpm.gov.uk

Plastic Window Federation
Construction House
85-87 Wellington Street
Luton
Bedfordshire
LU1 5AF
01582 456147
www.pwfed.co.uk

Royal Institute of Chartered
Surveyors
Directory of Member
Surveyors
www.dir.rics.org

Timber Research and
Development Council
01494 569600
www.trada.co.uk

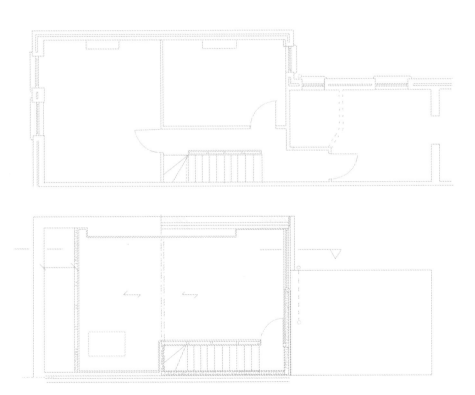

Index

agricultural restrictions 26
Approved Documents 32, 33, 35
Areas of Outstanding Natural
    Beauty 25, 26
Areas of Special Control 26
asbestos 159–60

balconies 80, 89
barns 142, 144–5
    conversion 13, 17, 142–69
    doors 145, 146
    floors 145, 148, 150–1
    to heat 165–9
    insulation 155–6
    retaining character of 144, 162
    roofs 142, 145, 152
    windows 146, 158, 163
basements
    bathrooms in 14, 106, 119
    conversion 13, 14–15, 25,
        104–23
    effect on parking space 30
    insulation 111–12
    ventilation 104, 106, 117
    windows 104
bathrooms 11, 160
    appliances 101
    in basement 14, 106, 119
    in loft 9, 65, 69, 85, 97, 98
    suites 100, 101
beams 66, 73
    flitch 59, 76–7
    metal lattice 74
    plywood box 74
    ridge 77
    steel 59, 65, 67, 74–5
    tie 77, 152–3
    timber 59, 75
bedrooms 9, 97, 98, 104
blinds 89, 101
blockwork skin 129–31
boilers
    combination 9, 98–9
    condensing 99–101
    location of 141
boundaries 13, 35, 37, 39
    to locate 39
bracing 142
Breach of Condition Notice 35
brickwork
    damaged 152

to protect 12–13
to render 159
to repoint 157
builders 9
    to choose 40–2
    contracts 46, 48, 50–1
    disputes with 43, 55–6
    estimates 44
    insurance 41, 42, 43
    payment 53–5
    quotations 40, 44, 45
    trade associations 40, 43
    warranties 43
    workmanship 48, 52, 55
Building Control: department 43,
        71, 80
    inspections 33–4, 35
    Officer 9, 31–2, 33, 55, 66,
        76, 77, 109
Building Notice 24, 34
Building Regulations 16, 17, 21,
        31–2, 33–4, 35, 52, 55,
        140, 167
    for double-glazing 126, 128
    exemption from 33
    fees 22–3, 24
    for insulation 90, 91, 92, 129
    for lofts 59, 65
    for stairs 8, 64, 79, 85
Building Warrant 24
bungalows 70, 78, 80, 82
    in France 71

cables
    in insulation 102, 161
    outdoor 164
ceiling 67, 80, 118, 120
    height 61, 62, 152
    joists 59, 76–7
central heating 98, 120–1
    see also radiators
change of use 31
chimneys 163, 167
circuit breakers 161, 163
cladding 12, 26, 138–9, 156,
        159
collars see beams, tie
colour: to choose 103, 122–3
completion certificate 34, 55
computers 102, 103
conservation areas 12–13, 25,
        26, 31, 62, 85, 87, 125,
        144
contamination 116–17

contingency sums 45
contract time 40, 54
contracts 46, 48, 50–1
council houses 26
covenants, restrictive 13, 27
credit agreements 54

damp 14, 91, 93, 107, 110,
        114, 131, 135, 151, 152
damp-proofing 14
    floors 107, 131
    liquid 115–16, 135
    outside 113–14
    walls 110–16, 151–2
daylight
    in basements 14, 104
    in garages 126, 128–9
    in lofts 85–6
daylight tube 14, 129
daywork rate 46
decorating
    basement 121–3
    loft 101, 103
designers 9
    agreeing terms 22
    to choose 16–17
    responsibility for risks 39
determination (DETR) 32–3
dining rooms 15
disputes
    with builders 43, 55–6
    with neighbours 37
drainage 7
    in basements 14, 113–15
    pumped system 7, 11, 14, 115
    shallow access 160–1
    shingle 135
drains 9
    to access 11
    land 113–14, 153
    to locate 11
dry-lining 111
dry rot 156–7

earth bonding 164
electrical distribution board 139,
        164
electrical work 69, 102, 118,
        139–41, 161–4
energy conservation/efficiency 32,
        52, 58, 89–90, 91–2, 112
entertainment rooms 15, 106,
        122
Environment Agency 13

Environmental Health Department 116, 117
environmental issues 94, 168-9

fascias 136
feasibility study 15, 22
finance 56-7
fire doors 64, 79
fire safety 35
  in basements 15, 104
  in lofts 8, 9, 59, 62-4, 65, 78-82, 87, 88
flooding 13, 14, 112-13
floors 14, 67, 69, 107-9
  barn 145, 148, 150-1
  floating 109, 112, 121
  to level 106-7, 108
  to lower 104, 109
  sound insulation in 94-6, 119
  timber 148, 150-1
  see also joists
foundations 7, 9, 37, 66, 69-71, 129, 147-8
fungal decay 156-7

garages
  conversion 13, 16, 25, 30, 37, 124-41
  illegal 35
  dimensions 124, 134
  insulation 128, 129-31, 138
  windows 126-9
gas supply 141
global warming 11, 13
grants 57-8, 100

headroom 8, 9, 20, 30, 60, 72, 77, 85, 91, 152
  in basements 104, 107, 109, 117
  on staircases 8, 20, 60
health and safety 32, 34, 35, 43, 52
  legislation 39
Health and Safety Executive 106
heating
  for barns 165-9
  for basements 120-1
home office/study 9, 31, 98, 102-3
hot-water supply 9, 98-101, 167
humidity 103

IEE wiring regulations 52, 102, 140, 141
inner skin
  blockwork 129-31
  timber 131-4
insect damage 155-6
insulation 15, 35, 58, 67, 69
  in barns 155-6
  in basements 111-12
  cables in 102, 161
  cavity-wall 93-4, 129-31
  exterior 134-5
  floor-grade 107, 108
  in garages 138, 129-31, 138
  materials 92-3, 93-4, 96, 131, 135
  sound 6, 7, 15, 89, 94-7, 98, 119
  thermal 32, 89-94, 128
insurance 41, 42, 43
invitation to tender 47, 48

joists
  ceiling 59, 76-7, 85, 95
  cripple 150
  floor 59, 65, 67, 68, 70, 73, 74, 75-6, 95, 97, 148
  span 74

kitchens 11, 14, 104, 120, 160, 165

ladder, fixed 8, 14, 85
Land Registry 13, 39
Lawful Development Certificate 25
layout
  floor 60-1
  of rooms 9, 15, 104, 105
letter of agreement 47, 48
lighting 14, 15, 118-20
  low-energy 119
  see also daylight
light-wells 104, 106
lintels 9, 66
Listed Building Consent 31
listed buildings 26, 31, 62, 87, 125
location plan 13
lofts
  bathrooms in 9, 65, 69, 85, 97, 98
  conversion 6-7, 8-9, 59-103
  effect on parking space 30
  exemption from Building

Regulations 33
  illegal 35, 76
  specialists in 41, 60
  structural design of 17
  floors 59, 67, 94-6, 97
  insulation 89-97
  windows 61-2, 67-8, 85-9

methane gas 116
mortar mixes 157, 158

National Parks 25, 26, 125
neighbours 27, 28, 29, 36-7, 39
  disputes with 37

off-street parking 25, 30, 124-5
  access to 125-6
Ombudsman, Local Authority 29
open fires 165, 167, 168
outbuilding conversion 13, 25
  of listed building 31
  see also barns
overlooking 29-30
overshading 29

packages, conversion 41, 60
parking, off-street 25, 30, 124-5
  access to 125-6
party walls 35-7, 93-4, 96
penalty clauses 54
permitted development
  quota 26
  rights 25-6, 31, 86
Planning Consent 25, 26, 31, 62, 124-6
  appeal 27-9
  applications 26-7, 30-1
  refusal 27, 28, 32
  retrospective 34-5
Planning Inspectorate 35
Planning Regulations 22-3
plans 18-21
  amendments 22, 23, 27, 32
playrooms 104, 106
plumbing 65, 67, 69, 98-101
power points 102, 164
Preservation Order 12
prime cost sums 45
privacy, invasion of 29-30
professional institutions 16-17
protected species 15, 39
  see also wildlife
provisional sums 45

purlins 8, 60

Quality Mark 44

racking resistance 142
radiators 103, 121, 165, 167
  electric 165
radon gas 116–17
rafters 59, 67, 68, 74, 77, 92,
  138, 156
rain damage 11–12
  see also weather resistance
regularisation certificate 35
repointing 157
risks, responsibility for 39
rooflights 9, 25, 59, 61, 62, 64,
  65, 67, 69, 85, 86, 89,
  103, 128–9, 146
  conservation-style 87, 146, 163
roofs
  barn 142, 145, 152
  coverings 135
  cut-and-pitched 8, 60, 77, 79,
    85
  flat 128, 135
  joists 8
  open 152
  pitch of 8, 61, 72, 88
  trussed-rafter 8, 60, 72, 79, 85
  trusses 6
  ventilation 91, 135–8

safety see health and safety
scale 30
Scottish legislation 24, 24, 56
self-closing devices 9, 64, 79
sequence of work 65–9
services
  in garage 139–41
  to locate 11
showers 100–1
site inspections 33–4
skylights see rooflights
smoke alarms 81–2, 102, 104
snagging 54–5
soffits 136–8
soil and vent pipe 7, 9, 14
solar pipe see daylight tube
solid-fuel heating 165, 167–8
space, illusion of 117–18
sprinklers 80–1
stairs/staircases 82–5
  in basements 14, 15, 104
  in bungalows 82

headroom for 8, 60, 82, 87
helical 14
lighting for 64, 86-7
to loft 8, 62-3, 65, 69, 82–5
paddle-tread 8, 14, 64, 84–5
position of 62, 64, 104
second 79
spiral 14
stairwell opening 14, 104
Standards, British 52–3, 116,
  148
storage 9, 15, 65, 97–8, 102–3,
  117
stoves 165, 167–8, 169
structural calculations 17, 22

tanking 110–16
  drainage cavity 110–11
  polyurethane resin 113
  see also damp-proofing
telephone points 102
thermal resistance 129
timber
  beams 59, 75
  cladding 138–9
  floors 148, 150–1
  inner skin 131–4
  to repair 158–9, 163
Town and Country Planning Act
  25, 26
trees 12–13, 148

underfloor heating 120-1, 165
underpinning 69–71, 148
utility rooms 14, 106, 120

vapour-permeable sheets 131
variation orders 45–6
VAT 44
ventilation 14, 35, 62, 103, 165
  in basements 104, 106, 117
  extractor 14, 106, 119
  roof 91, 135–8
  underfloor 150–1

walls
  ashlare 59, 61, 67, 77, 97, 102
  heights 75
  cavity 93–4, 129, 131, 135
  to damp-proof 110–16
  to finish 120, 134
  insulation 93–4, 96–7,
    111–12
  load-bearing 7, 70, 71, 72

party 35–7, 93–4, 96
  sleeper 151
  to strengthen 129
  stud partition 69, 72, 97,
    132–3, 146, 165
  to upgrade 129–34
water main 7
water pipes 141
water tanks 64–5, 67
WC 11, 160
weather resistance 11–12, 35,
  72, 129, 131, 134, 135,
  139, 157, 158, 159
wet rot 156, 157
wildlife 13, 15, 39, 169
windows
  in barns 146, 158, 163
  in basements 104
  dormer 8, 9, 25, 26, 29, 35,
    61–2, 65, 67–8, 69, 73,
    82, 85–6, 89, 91
  in garages 126–9
  position of 87, 88–9
  see also rooflights
woodwork, to repair 158–9, 163